An OBSERVATION SURVEY of Early Literacy Achievement

An OBSERVATION SURVEY of Early Literacy Achievement

THIRD EDITION

MARIE M. CLAY

The Marie Clay
Literacy Trust

An Observation Survey of Early Literacy Achievement

© 2013 The Marie Clay Literacy Trust
First published 1993, 2nd edition 2002
Reprinted 2002 (twice), 2003, 2005 (with updated US stanines), 2007, 2008, 2009 (x3), 2010 (x5), 2011 (x2), 2012
Revised 3rd edition 2013
Reprinted 2014, 2015 (twice), 2016, 2017

ISBN NZ 978-1-4860-1260-2
ISBN USA 978-0-325-04901-4
ISBN UK 978-1-407-15991-1

Global Education Systems [GES] Ltd
5/32 St Stephens Avenue, Parnell, Auckland 1052, New Zealand
www.globaled.co.nz

Distributed by

United States: Heinemann, 361 Hanover Street, Portsmouth, NH 03801-3912
www.heinemann.com

Australia: Scholastic Australia Pty Ltd, PO Box 579, Gosford, NSW 2250
ABN 11 000 614 577
www.scholastic.com.au

New Zealand: Scholastic New Zealand Ltd, Private Bag 94407, Botany, Auckland 2163
www.scholastic.co.nz

UK and Eire by Scholastic Ltd, Book End, Range Road, Witney, Oxfordshire OX29 0YD
www.scholastic.co.uk/marieclay

Printed in China by Nordica

Library of Congress Cataloguing-in Publication Data
Clay, Marie M.
An observation survey of early literacy achievement / by Marie M. Clay — revised 2nd ed.
p. cm.
Includes bibliographical references and index
ISBN: 978- 0-325-04901-4 (US)
ISBN: 978-1-4860-1260-2 (NZ)
1. Reading (Primary)—Ability testing—New Zealand
2. Reading (Primary)—New Zealand
3. English language—Composition and exercises—Study and teaching (Primary)—New Zealand
4. English language—Composition and exercises—Ability testiin—New Zealand
5. Observation (Educational method) I. Title
LB1525.C56 2005
372.4'049—dc22   2005033541

The pronouns 'she' and 'he' have often been used in this text to refer to the teacher and child respectively. Despite a possible charge of sexist bias it makes for clearer, easier reading if such references are consistent.

Preface to the third edition

The preparation of this third edition of *An Observation Survey of Early Literacy Achievement* has resulted from the collaboration of The Marie Clay Literacy Trust with the International Reading Recovery Trainers Organisation (IRRTO), the association of educators who provide leadership for all entities affiliated with Reading Recovery internationally. The international Trainers and a substantial number of Tutors/Teacher Leaders from each country with Reading Recovery, were surveyed to inform the editing process.

To secure updated assessment statistics and reports of new studies of test reliability and validity of the Observation Survey tasks, a number of researchers studying Reading Recovery in their respective countries were invited to contribute relevant data. Their work makes significant contributions to this revision. The final part of the process involved an international set of Reading Recovery professionals, identified by the IRRTO Executive Board, reviewing the text prior to publication. The careful reading they undertook served as an important, final edit of this edition.

The work on the third edition of *An Observation Survey of Early Literacy Achievement* was completed with the input and contributions of:

- An editorial/production team in Auckland, including Rosalie Lockwood, Graham McEwan, Barbara Watson, Sam Hill and Vincent Reynolds;

- Members of the IRRTO Executive Board, including Susan Bodman, Christine Boocock, Connie Briggs, Janice Farmer Hailey, and Janice Van Dyke;

- Members of the IRRTO Communications Committee, including Salli Forbes and Patricia Scharer for conducting surveys and compiling results;

- Researchers whose work contributed new norms, correlations, and reliability coefficients, including Irene Huggins, Allyson Matczuk, Jeden Tolentino, and J. Kniskern of Canada; Andrew J. Holliman, Jane Hurry, and Julia Douëtil of the United Kingdom, and Jerome D'Agostino of the United States;

- Members of IRRTO who served with the Executive Board members as editorial reviewers who read and commented on the final draft: Billie Askew, Julia Douëtil, Elizabeth Kaye, Claire Marshall, Allyson Matczuk, and Heather Turpin.

In summary, the publication of this text represents an extensive effort involving The Marie Clay Literacy Trust, an international set of Reading Recovery professionals led by IRRTO, and key researchers involved in recent studies around the Observation Survey. All worked collaboratively to maintain Marie Clay's valued, original Observation Survey and to enhance its relevance with appropriate updates.

Mary Anne Doyle, Consulting Editor
The Marie Clay Literacy Trust

Contents

Supporting teaching resources

An Observation Survey: The Video (DVD) (Koefoed and Watson, 1999) is designed to supplement a careful reading of these observation procedures. Two teachers administer the Observation Survey to two children, providing a visual resource to assist viewers to understand the standard ways of administering and scoring these six observation tasks.

An Observation Survey, The Video: Guidenotes (Koefoed, Boocock and Wood, 1999) provides examples of how the recording sheets for the tasks may be used to record, score, and comment on the responses of two children.

An Observation Survey Copymasters are available for the record sheets that are contained in this book.

Introduction

I have worked as a teacher of young children, a special education teacher, a school psychologist, and a teacher of school psychologists. I have also carried out research in developmental psychology, and as part of that research I have observed how children change over time as they learn more and more from all their various environments. I have observed both children who make good progress and children who find learning difficult.

My work has produced some systematic observation measurement tasks that are used widely in New Zealand and in other countries and that have been reported in the research literature. These tasks help teachers to observe:

- the child's use of oral language and how he controls sentence structures and inflections of words

- concepts about print (how print encodes information)

- the reading of continuous text (taking a Running Record)

- letter knowledge

- reading vocabulary (words the child knows when reading)

- writing vocabulary (words the child knows when writing)

- hearing and recording sounds in words (both phonemic awareness and the linking of phonemes to letters).

While there are many other kinds of systematic observation, such as the retelling of stories (McKenzie, 1989; Morrow, 1989; Ministry of Education SEA test, 1997), and approaches to more advanced story writing, I have limited the account in this book to the observation tasks which arose from my own research.

An Observation Survey of Early Literacy Achievement describes some observation tasks that have guided teachers in New Zealand for many decades in their teaching of young children in formal school programmes (Department of Education, 1985; Ministry of Education, 1996, 2003). I will discuss the various ways in which these observations can be made, as well as why they must be made during the child's first years of school.

For whom is this book written?

This book is for teachers who want to be careful observers of how young children learn to read and write. The observation tasks capture some of the rapid change that occurs in early literacy awareness. Teachers can observe how children differ one from another, and how individual children make the transition from preschool into formal schooling in different ways. Sensitive assessments can be made with these tasks well before standardised group tests are able to measure across the wide range of prior achievements that teachers find in their classes.

An Observation Survey of Early Literacy Achievement will be of assistance to teachers who work with a variety of literacy programmes and will enable them to monitor the progress of their children. However, it is especially useful for those teachers who are not restricted to a sequenced curriculum. When teachers themselves determine the sequence of instruction, using projects or topics, or integrated curricular activities, these kinds of observation procedures are essential.

This book is also for teachers who work individually with children having temporary difficulties with literacy learning. It is for administrators who want their teachers to give them easy-to-read accounts of individual progress made by children between two specific points of time. It is for students who are learning about early literacy behaviours and who are training themselves to be observers of learners. And it is for researchers who wish to determine how young children learn to read and write, because these observation tasks have sound measurement qualities.

To use systematic observation the teacher has to set time aside from teaching to become a neutral observer.

Training should precede any attempts to use the observation tasks. Teachers who try to use them by relying solely on the written account in this book are not likely to find as much value in them as teachers who are able to discuss what comes from the observations with colleagues, for in such discussion the reader can test his or her understanding of the text against the (possible) meanings intended by the author.

Behind these observations there are theoretical rationales

The observation tasks reported in this book are derived from a theory of how young children come to master the complex tasks of reading and writing continuous text (Clay, 1991, 1998, 2001).

Despite my training in the measurement field, and my experience in clinical child psychology, I have come to regard normative, standardised tests as having a place in education, but only as an indirect way for teachers to obtain information about students' learning. When compared with the observation of learners at work, test scores are mere approximations or estimates that do not provide good guidance to the teacher of how to teach a particular child. At times those scores present results stripped of the very information that is required for designing or evaluating sound instruction for individual learners. Standardised tests need to be supplemented at the classroom level with systematic observations of children who are in the act of responding to instruction, observations that are reliable enough to compare one child with another, or one child on two different occasions.

When a child learns language, he works on his own theories about how things work and changes those theories as he comes into contact with clear evidence to the contrary. What I like about observation is that it allows us to watch the child as he works, to see at least part of the focus of his attention, to watch him search for information in print and for confirmation of what he thinks. It enables us to watch him solve a problem and sometimes express his delight when he discovers something new.

Consequently, during the first two years of schooling, and in particular for programmes that encourage children to read and write texts which are not part of a prescriptive curriculum, observation records are more useful than the estimates of standardised tests or the intuitions of informal/casual observations. The systematic observations that are needed call for the teacher to take a closer look than she normally has the time to take. They inform the teaching process, the parents and the administrators. They can feed data into the analyses of researchers. Best of all, they provide evidence of learning on repeated measurements on tasks like the ones the child is actually undertaking in the classroom. *In every way the information produced by systematic observation reduces our uncertainties and improves our instruction* (see Clay, 2001, pages 268–276).

Marie M. Clay

1 Observing change in early literacy behaviours

An introduction to systematic observation

Observation of what goes on in classrooms has uncovered differences in the time allocated to children and activities. This shows clearly that high progress children get a greater number of opportunities to learn than low progress children. Studies of how successful children learn show them getting better and better at literacy tasks as they draw away from average or below average children whose progress occurs at an apparently slower rate. However, one reason for this slow rate of learning could be that children are not getting the kinds of help they need to learn at a faster pace.

Observing individual progress

If we attend to individual children as they work, and if we focus on the progressions in learning that occur over time, our detailed observations can provide feedback to our instruction. Carefully recorded observations can lead us to modify our instruction to meet the learning needs of particular children in the formative stages of new learning, like beginning reading, beginning writing and beginning mathematics.

Planned observations can capture evidence of early progress. All science is based on systematic observation of phenomena under known conditions. Physicists or chemists in laboratories, botanists and zoologists in the field, and behavioural scientists in psychology, sociology, linguistics and cultural anthropology all use observation to gather research data, but in each of those subjects the observation takes place under strictly controlled conditions. In the past it was not easy to convince teachers that observing individual children at work was a legitimate part of literacy teaching and assessment. Today, despite some lingering mistrust, direct observation in research about young learners is not only acceptable but has a complementary role to play alongside other research and assessment approaches. It is particularly useful for children up to eight or nine years of age (Genishi, 1982).

Assessment

Measuring outcomes

Historically, most educational assessment has been directed to the outcomes of instruction. We wait until the end of the instruction sequence before we assess. Then:

- we monitor national effectiveness

- we assess school effectiveness

- we assess teacher effectiveness

- we assess primary (elementary) school outcomes

- we assess high school outcomes.

When we use tests to measure the outcomes of teaching, the instruction of the learners is already over. In legal terms, we would say that the test score comes 'after the fact'. Based on what these scores reveal it is almost too late to change the fate of students. We no longer have the chance to do that; the opportunity has gone.

Educators have come to rely mainly on systematic testing of outcomes rather than systematic observation of learning. The measurement strategies used to develop tests and to guide research analyses led us towards sound interpretations of tests, but as we improved our standardised tests we also deprived teachers and administrators of valuable information about how learners were learning. There is something seductive in the efficiency of final assessment scores. Yet in the periods leading up to these final assessments, children learn things every day. In education, we also need to evaluate the progress of learners as they make their way towards those final assessments. A class teacher needs to be aware of the individual progress of each learner over time in a particular programme, especially when the learners are young and when a new subject is being introduced to novice learners.

Of course we need research which looks for explanations of what causes what, or what conditions bring about differences. The answers to such questions call for the use of a variety of research paradigms for testing and analysing data, but for effective instruction we also need answers to two basic questions.

- What typically occurs for the children we teach while learning is taking place during the time between assessments?

- How is this individual child changing over time in relation to what typically occurs?

Teachers who have answers to these questions will be better able to adapt the daily instruction of their pupils. Observations of a standard kind provide the teacher with appropriate feedback (see page 12).

Measures of outcomes tell us about the achievement levels of the education system. Such assessments do not tell us what led to those achievement levels. We do not know from the assessments how the high achievement levels were obtained, or why there are low achievement levels. If we try to use those results to improve instruction:

- we can only guess how to change our teaching

- we can only guess how to change our policies.

We do not have to test all children to assess educational standards at the national, state, or district level; we can use sampling methods to get information on standards in the same way that we conduct public opinion polls. We do not need to test every child to know whether the school system is producing satisfactory outcomes. In many countries there is some agreement that this assessment of the education system can be done best from the age of nine years and upwards.

Measuring abilities

Measurement theory has allowed us to measure the abilities of individual learners (their intelligence, language skills, auditory and visual perception, and so on). When we measure these things we **predict** how well a particular student might learn in our programmes. This type of testing is usually administered prior to instruction and it has resulted in children being grouped according to estimated abilities.

Even when we give these tests to individuals we score them according to what we know happens to groups of children. We predict for individuals from **group** data, not from **individual** data. We use norms, or average scores for children of the same age. Such predictions often prove to be wrong for individual children.

If teachers do use outcome tests and ability scores, and many will be required to do so, they should be aware that every expectation they hold of what a child can and cannot learn should be mistrusted. This means that they should make an hypothesis that they are willing to revise. If we give the learner particular opportunities and different learning conditions, he might prove the test's predictions to be wrong. Teachers should always be ready to be surprised by any child.

Every test score has some error of measurement attached to it; there is error in group scores, and error in individual scores. We should keep an open mind about what is possible for the individual child to achieve. We have in the past made assumptions about children that have closed the door on further opportunities to learn.

Whenever our predictions for particular children are wrong, teaching practices tend to deprive those children of learning opportunities. We exclude them from certain opportunities or challenges.

- We keep them out of school.

- Or we hold them back to repeat the same class with the same curriculum.

- Or we give them less to learn.

- Or we give them radically simplified tasks.

Very young children have usually been studied using direct observation (in developmental psychology). Early childhood educators had to use observations of what children can do because little children often cannot put into words what they are doing or thinking, and they cannot complete paper and pencil questionnaires. Studies of how children learn to speak have been exciting, and so have some of the studies of what children are learning as they learn to read and write. However teachers must go beyond reactions like 'Ooh! Ah!' or 'I am surprised!' and 'Isn't that cute!', and try to understand what is happening as individual children learn.

Assessments that guide our teaching

Effective teaching calls for a third kind of assessment designed to record how the child works on tasks. Teachers can then progressively modify their teaching accordingly. Compare this to a football game: the quality of the team play is not improved by looking at the final score. The coach must look closely at how the team is playing the game and help the players to use strategic moves which produce a better final score.

When the class teacher observes how individual children are problem-solving, it makes a difference to what happens in classrooms. Such observations are particularly useful in three kinds of situations:

- for young children up to eight years of age

- at the introduction of new kinds of learning

- when the activity being learned is complex.

Classroom teachers can observe students as they construct responses by moving among them as they work. They can observe how individuals change over time by keeping good records; and they can allow children to take different learning paths to the same outcomes because they are clearly aware of the learning that is occurring.

Such teachers are like craftspeople, monitoring how their products take shape. Think of the painter or potter adjusting the light, shade, colour, shape or texture of a product in formation. Or we could think of the violinist in the orchestra who knows that one of his strings is slipping off pitch. He takes an opportunity during a pause in the performance to avert disaster by tightening the string. He would not wait for the critic's review of the performance in the morning paper, saying one violin was out of tune! Skilled craftspeople fine-tune the ongoing construction or performance. Teaching involves making on-the-run adjustments of this kind.

To improve teaching, teachers need to observe children's responses as they learn to read and write and watch for:

- competencies and confusions

- strengths and weaknesses

- evidence of processing and strategic activities

- evidence of what the child can already control.

Observing oral language

Studies of how children learn to speak have produced exciting results. In the 1960s researchers went into homes to observe children learning language and record its use as it occurred in natural settings. They followed the progress of individual children as they developed and as their language changed. They studied what actually occurred, making precise records, and they did not depend on tests or on recollections of what occurred (Brown, 1973; Paley, 1981; Wells, 1986; Hart and Risley, 1999).

Researchers' interest shifted from an early focus on the structures of language to the meanings of language. In the 1970s this evolution led us to study the effects of the contexts in which language occurs. The young child's language is so related to the things he is talking about that you can have trouble understanding him unless you also know about the things he refers to. We became more sensitive to the ways in which we change our language according to the place we are in, and who we are talking to. We have learned more about the ways in which the languages of the homes differ, more about dialects, and more about the complexities of bilingual learning.

Attention moved to the detailed study of interactions between mothers and children, teachers and children, children and children. As a result of all this recording of naturally occurring behaviour we now know a great deal more about the ways in which the contexts of language interactions facilitate or constrain the development of language in children. We know that entry into formal education settings such as schools reduces children's opportunities for talking. And we know how schooling can prevent children from using the language which they used so effectively before they came to school (Cazden, 2001).[*]

Observing emerging literacy

Since the mid-1970s there have been some interesting observational studies of children's writing. The young child has emerged as an active participant in the process of becoming a writer. Studies of Mexican and Argentinian children (Ferreiro and Teberosky, 1982; Vernon and Ferreiro, 1999, 2000) describe the fascinating shifts that occur well before children begin to use the alphabetical principle of letter-sound relationships, which we commonly think of as the beginning of writing. These preschool children were making discoveries about writing, and were trying to construct writing systems. The observation of early writing behaviours has taken us forward in great leaps. We learned a great deal about the years of development before these children might be able to take a spelling test and get a few items correct!

---

[*] Reading about the *Record of Oral Language* (Clay et al., 2007) and *Classroom Discourse* (Cazden, 2001), or a standard story-retelling task (McKenzie, 1989; Morrow, 1989), or the 'Tell Me' sub-test designed by S. McNaughton for the New Zealand School Entry Assessment (Ministry of Education, 1997) would sensitise teachers to individual differences in children's growing control over constructing stories.

Many observers discovered that preschool children explore the detail of print in their environment, on signs, cereal packets and television advertisements. They develop concepts about books, newspapers and messages, and learn a little about what it is to read these. Case studies over long periods of time show how more advanced concepts emerge out of earlier understandings.

Preschool children already know something about the world of print from their environments. This leads them to form primitive hypotheses about letters, words or messages both printed and handwritten. It is a widely held view that learning to read and write in school will be easier for the child with rich preschool literacy experiences than it is for the child who has had few opportunities for such learning.

We have learned of these things mainly through research which has used observation rather than experimentation as its method of enquiry. When we become neutral observers and watch children at work in systematic and repeatable ways we begin to uncover some of our own assumptions and notice how wrong these can sometimes be.

Observing school entrants

Systematic observation of school entrants has distinct advantages over 'readiness testing'. By the time children enter school they have been learning for five to six years. Every child is ready to learn more than he or she already knows. Why do schools and educators find this so difficult to understand? Teachers must find out what children already know, and take them from where they are to somewhere else.

When we give a readiness test to a new school entrant we are trying to predict school progress from what a child already knows (see Measuring abilities, pages 6–7). We are merely asking 'Are you ready for my programme?' Readiness tests divide children into two groups: a competent group ready to learn on a particular programme and a problem group supposedly not ready for this type of learning. On the other hand, observations which record what any learner already knows about emerging literacy eliminate the problem group. *All children are ready to learn something*, but some start their learning from a different place. Not many teachers of school entrants are able to assess which five-year-olds have only the literacy experience of two- or three-year-olds.

Suppose we observe the literacy behaviours of a group of new school entrants. Some know a few things about reading and writing and others know very little. Those who know very little may have paid almost no attention to print in their preschool years because they had little opportunity or encouragement to do so, or because they had no incentive or interest. Perhaps some adults around them tried to teach them to read and write and the children found the tasks very confusing and so gave up on trying to learn. Undoubtedly, what the young child knows about literacy when he or she enters school is not a matter of competency unfolding from within, since in an oral culture where literacy does not exist, no such behaviour unfolds. It is a matter of having the opportunity to learn how to use a very arbitrary symbol system.

There will be individual differences for other reasons but there is one aspect of this development that we can influence and foster: we can provide appropriate opportunities for the child to learn. That usually means providing a responsive environment within which the child can explore and negotiate meanings.

When children enter school we need to observe what they know and can do, and build on that foundation whether it is rich or meagre.

The New Zealand teachers with whom I worked in various research projects did observe children when they entered school and set out to expand outwards from the various competencies that children already had. The teachers taught in ways that introduced children to print in reading and writing activities so that they could learn more than they already knew. Teachers gave more help and more attention to the children who knew the least; they did not set them aside to 'ripen' on their own. They considered their job was to make up for missed opportunities for learning.

The observation tasks used in this survey are *not* readiness tests which sort children according to whether they are ready to learn or not. In particular the Concepts About Print (C.A.P.) task is not a readiness test because it samples only one dimension of a child's preparation for formal instruction. However, 'in the United States … the C.A.P. tests have tended to be used in kindergarten in much the same way that readiness tests are often used' (Stallman and Pearson, 1990). These authors anticipated the construction of better commercially available tests of readiness.

I think we should abandon the readiness concept. All children are ready to learn more than they already know; it is the teachers who need to know how to create appropriate instruction for each child, whatever his or her starting point. To do this effectively they need to observe how literacy behaviours change throughout the first years of school. (See also Clay, 1991.)

My analyses of beginning reading and writing tell me that children have to extend their knowledge along each of several different dimensions of learning as they approach formal literacy instruction. At the same time they have to learn how to relate learning in any one of these areas (say letter learning) to learning in any other (say messages and meanings). Along each of these dimensions more learning has to occur. It does not happen in an orderly way. It is not the same for all children. Each learner starts with what he or she already knows and uses that to support what has to be learnt next.

To become observers of the early stages of literacy learning teachers will have to give up looking for a single, short assessment test for the acquisition stages of reading and writing. Children move into reading by different tracks and early assessments must be wide-ranging. If there is a single task that stands up better than any other it is the Running Record of text reading. This is a neutral observation task, capable of use in any system of reading, and recording progress on whatever gradient of text difficulty has been adopted by the education system. (See pages 51–83; also Johnston, 1996, 2000.)

Standardised tests are poor measures of slow progress

It is difficult and perhaps impossible to design good measurement tools for use close to the onset of instruction. Standardised tests sample from all behaviours and they do not discriminate well until considerable progress has been made by many of the children (Clay, 1991, page 204). Yet if you ask teachers to identify young children making slow progress they can do this fairly accurately earlier than standardised tests can do so in reliable ways. In my own research 20 to 25 percent of beginning readers were showing some confusions and difficulties 12 to 18 months before good assessments could be obtained from standardised tests. The children were at the tail end of the distribution of test scores, moving very slowly up from zero scores. Systematic observation by teachers is an alternative way to achieve early identification of children who need supplementary help.

For similar reasons age or grade level scores are not very satisfactory indicators of progress in the first years of school. Because children enter school with very different knowledge about reading and writing, assessments on standard measures of performance are not very informative. Most low-achieving children would have zero to low scores for long periods. I would want to have, in addition, records of the small amounts of progress made by individual children — where they were at various points during the year, how they work on the problems they find in texts, and what processes they could apply to what texts.

Observational data must be as reliable as test data to be acceptable as evidence (see Appendix 2, pages 166–173). Running Records have been shown to be a highly reliable way of measuring accuracy and error (reliability r = 0.98). Observers find it more difficult to agree on self-correction behaviours (r = 0.68).

The data from Running Records of text reading have both face and content validity. If you can say a child can read the book that you want him to read at a given level of competency little or nothing is being inferred. You can count the number of correct words to get an accuracy score. While the record does not give a measure of something labelled comprehension you can assess this subjectively by recording the child's responses to your asking about the story, and you can analyse errors and self-corrections to find out how well the child works for meaning. You will not get a score for how many letters the child knows, but you can see whether the child uses his letter knowledge on the run in his reading.

In summary, standardised tests are indirect ways of observing children's progress. They are suitable for analysing the behaviours of groups of children but cannot compare with the observation of learners at work for providing the information needed to design sound instruction. On the other hand the units of measurement in the observation tasks are immediately transferrable to teaching interventions because they direct a teacher's attention to precisely what it is that she needs to teach.

Systematic observation of learners

Educators have done a great deal of systematic testing and relatively little systematic observation of learning. One could argue that educators need to give most of their attention to the systematic observation of learners who are on the way to those final scores on tests. Systematic observations have four characteristics in common with good measurement instruments. They provide:

- a standard task

- a standard way of administering the task

- ways of knowing when we can rely on our observations and make valid comparisons

- a task that is like a real world task as a guarantee that the observations will relate to what the child is likely to do in the real world (for this establishes the validity of the observation).

Together, a standard task with standard administration and with standard scoring procedures provide sound measurement conditions. Otherwise we would be evaluating with a piece of stretchy measuring tape instead of using an instrument that behaves in the same way on every occasion. Two measurements with a stretchy tape cannot be compared; and comparability is often important not only at the national, state and district level but at the individual level. Watching the progress of children we often want reliable ways to compare a student on two of his own performances. A standard task, which is administered and scored in a standard way, gives one kind of guarantee of reliability when we make such comparisons.

Not all of our observations have to be on standard tasks but those used to demonstrate change over time should be. The problem with observations is that they can have some sources of error not found in standardised tests. One of these sources of 'error' is that what the observer 'knows' about reading and writing will determine what that observer is likely to observe in children's literacy development. You bring to the observation what you already believe. Observers must be aware of this and try to correct for it. All teachers using the tasks in *An Observation Survey of Early Literacy Achievement* should be trained in how to administer, score and interpret their results in reliable ways.

When important decisions are to be made we should increase the range of observations we make in order to decrease the risk of making errors in our interpretations. We need to design procedures that limit the possibilities of being in error or being misled by what we observe. That is why, in the rest of this book, space is given to the precautions that observers must take if they wish to gather valid records. It is also why a wide range of measures or observations should be made. *No one technique is sufficiently reliable on its own.*

An unreliable test score means that if you took other measures, at around the same time or at another time, you might get very different results. We have to be concerned with whether our assessments are reliable because we do not want to alter our teaching, or decide on a child's placement, on the basis of a flawed judgement. We need to be able to rely on the data from which we make our judgements.

For example, a word test should never be used in isolation because it assesses only one aspect of early reading behaviours. So does retelling. The child is learning more about letters, how print is written down, how to form letters and write words, and something about letter-sound relationships. Teachers need to know how learning is proceeding in each of these areas. That is why the observation tasks described in this survey range across each of these areas of knowledge.

It is important that we use tasks that are 'authentic'. The word authentic has arisen among educators because many tests of reading and writing and spelling are being challenged as non-valid measures of real world literacy activities. One of the criticisms of the multiple choice type of test items is that they are a special type of task not found in real life; they are a test device with no real world reference. It will be better if we can find sound assessment procedures which reflect what the learner is mastering or struggling to master. (Concepts About Print was designed to have such authenticity 20 years before that word appeared in the assessment field.)

Characteristics of observation tasks

All the observation tasks in *An Observation Survey of Early Literacy Achievement* were developed in research studies. I like to call them observation tasks but they do have the qualities of sound assessment instruments with reliability and validity and discrimination indices established in research. Theories of measurement and other theories were taken into account in the design of these observation tasks: I drew upon evidence from the psychology of learning, from developmental psychology, from studies of individual differences, and from theories about social factors and the influence of contexts on learning.

The observation tasks were not designed to produce samples of work which go into portfolios; they were designed to make a teacher attend to how children work at learning in the classroom. It is useful to supplement our observations of children's products in a portfolio with systematic observation tasks, because portfolio products are often channelled by the teacher's ways of teaching or their expectations. Sometimes a different kind of observation task will confront the teacher with a new kind of evidence of a child's strengths or problems.

The observation tasks in this survey do not simplify the learning challenge. They are designed to allow children to work with the complexities of written language. They do not measure children's general abilities, and they do not look for the outcomes of a particular programme. They tell teachers something about how the learner searches for information in printed texts and how that learner works with that information.

2 Reading and writing: processing the information in print

The reading process

Reading, like thinking, is a complex process. The reader has to produce responses to the words the author wrote. In some way the reader has to match his or her thinking to that of the author. Good readers reduce their uncertainty about what they are reading by asking themselves very effective questions as they read; they know when they are more or less on-track. On the other hand, poor readers ask themselves rather trivial questions and waste their opportunities to reduce their uncertainty. They do not put the information-seeking processes into effective sequences.

Many instructional programmes direct their students to the trivial questions. They do not mean to confuse children but they do, by oversimplifying and stressing particular parts of the reading process. All readers, be they five-year-old beginners working on their first books or effective adult readers, need to find and use different kinds of information in print and combine the information they find with what they carry in their heads from their past experiences with language. What kinds of information must be used? Included are:

- knowledge of how the world works

- the possible meanings of the text

- the sentence structures of the language

- rules about the order of ideas, or words, or letters

- the words used often in the language

- the alphabet

- special features of sound, shape and layout

- special knowledge about books and literary experiences.

Readers work on several of these features and 'correct reading' is a perfect match with the author's text on all the features. The terms 'look and say' or 'sight words' or 'phonics' are used to describe some recommended 'methods of instruction' which are over-simplified accounts of what we actually need to learn to do in order to be able to read.

When the reader reads for meaning, he is finding and using information from many sources. After only one year of instruction the high progress reader can pull many different kinds of information together to read accurately. When he reads, he appears to focus on the meaning of the text. If he anticipates something about structure (for example as he turns the page) this can be checked by a rapid search with his eyes which picks up visual information, triggers sound-to-letter associations (or letter-to-sound associations) or clusters of letters and words already known. The high progress six-year-old has several ways of functioning according to the type of reading material or the difficulty level of the material. If he cannot get the meaning with fast recall of known words he shifts to using slower analyses of words, letter clusters and letters. If the first things he notices are some letters, he makes some letter-to-sound links to solve the words which become chunked in phrases to get to messages. He will use his knowledge of words to get to new words and he will also use his knowledge of letter clusters or letter-sound associations to unpick new words. This does not work too well unless he already 'knows' the word in his speaking vocabulary. Throughout this entire flexible process, the competent reader manages to stay focused on the messages conveyed by the text, while unpicking the detailed information stored in the print on the page.

On the other hand, a low progress reader or a reader at risk of having difficulty learning to read tends to operate slowly on a narrow range of weak processes. He may rely on making up the story from some memory of the book and pay only slight attention to visual details. He may disregard obvious discrepancies between his response and the words on the page. He may be looking so hard for words he knows and guessing words from first letters that he forgets what the message is about. Such primitive ways of operating on print can easily become established habits if they are practised day after day, and the habits become very resistant to change. For some children this is what happens in the first year of formal instruction.

That is why systematic observation of what the child can do and where his new learning is taking him is so important in the first year of school. Close and individual attention from a teacher at this stage can help children to operate on print in more efficient ways, so that potential low progress readers come to function like the high progress readers. If that does not happen they do not learn to work effectively under normal classroom conditions and they may never make progress at average rates.

In recent years there have been shifts in our understanding of some psychological processes and yet old theories remain encapsulated in our teaching methods and assumptions. Some of these shifts need to be reviewed here. The most important challenge for the teacher of reading is to change the ways in which the child operates on print to get to the messages.

We must look briefly at the model of the reading process that is implied. (A more extensive discussion related to the early years of formal schooling is available in Clay, 1991, 1998, 2001.)

1   *Reading involves messages expressed in language.* Usually that language is a special kind of language found in books. Although some children may not use the same oral language dialect as that used by the teacher or the reading books, children will have a well-developed language system and will communicate well in their homes and communities. They will control most of the sounds of the language and a large vocabulary of words, which are labels for quite complex sets of meanings, and they will have flexible ways of constructing sentences. However, the spoken language dialect differs in important ways from the written language dialect they will find in their reading books.

2   *Reading also involves knowing about the conventions used to print language* — directional rules, space formats, and punctuation signals for new sentences, new speakers, surprise or emphasis, and questions. These are things which the skilled reader does not think about: he responds giving only minimal attention to such conventions of print. But beginning readers have to learn the directional 'road rules' for print, for these rules determine the order of what you must attend to in print. Ignoring the signals of layout and punctuation will lead to some fundamental confusions. (See Clay, 2010b.)

3   *Reading involves visual patterns — groups of words, word parts, clusters of letters and single letters*, depending on how one wants to break up the visual patterns. Processing information from the printed page is very fast in skilled readers. In experiments we can show how adults scan text to pick up patterns or clusters of letters but only when we drastically alter the reading situation. Luckily young children operate on visual patterns slowly enough for us to observe some of what they do.

4   *Reading involves listening to language and hearing clear breaks between words.* Young children have some difficulty breaking messages up into words. They have even greater difficulty breaking up a word into its sequence of sounds and hearing the sounds in sequence. This is not strange. Some of us have the same problem with the note sequences in a complicated melody.

That list introduces four different areas of learning which facilitate progress in reading. Language was discussed first because the meanings embodied in print are of high utility: it is easier to read a text when one already knows something about the topic. Language provides powerful sources of information for literacy activities. One important source is the meanings of words, phrases, sentences and texts, and another lies in the structures of the sentences. A less reliable and sometimes confusing and distorting source of information for the young reader lies in the letter-sound relationships. However, theoretical analyses tell us that there are consistencies in the letter-to-sound relationships and regularities of the spelling patterns or clusters of letters, both of which assist the mature reader's reading. The human brain is well-designed to search for and find such regularities, and make use of them. Debate still surrounds letter-to-sound and the sound-to-letter relationships, and in particular how this should be taught to beginning readers.

The conventions used by printers to print language also need to be learned because we need to attend to the visual information in the order laid out in the printer's code, more or less. You can scan a picture in any direction you like but print is laid out in an order which must be followed by the reader.

Visual information is essential for fluent correct responding and skilled readers tend to use visual knowledge in a highly efficient way, scanning at several levels in order to check on the messages of the text. The beginning reader must discover for himself how to do this scanning and how to visually analyse print to locate features that distinguish between letters and words.

The sound sequences in words (which linguists call the sequences of phonemes) are also used in rapid reading, perhaps to anticipate a word in peripheral vision (out to the right in English) and to check any word the reader is uncertain about. This requires the reader to use two kinds of detailed and carefully synchronised analysis: the analysis of sounds in sequence and left-to-right visual analysis with appropriate return sweeps at the end of lines.

Most children can become literate if the conditions for learning are right for them. Three shifts in knowledge about learning have raised our expectations for greater success for more children in literacy learning today.

- First, it is accepted now that experience counts in cognitive functioning, and some of what we thought of as 'given' in intelligence is learned during the process of cognitive development.

- Secondly, there has been a shift away from the belief that 'in some rough and ready way' achievement matches to general measured intelligence. We have known for decades that when you look at the children who are over-achieving, for example when a child is reading well and several years above his mental age level, then the supposed match between achievement and intelligence must be questioned.

If we put those two concepts together — that some part of the cognitive process is learned or realised through experience and that achievement ages do not necessarily match mental ages — there is plenty of scope for teaching and learning experience to bring about a change in children's attainments.

- Thirdly, another shift of knowledge has been in the area of brain functioning. When psychologists wrote about the brain as similar to a telephone exchange, association theories of learning were popular and people were thought of as having better or poorer telephone exchanges, pre-wired to do better or poorer jobs. Without discarding the idea that people may differ in the brain structures they have to work with, it is now known that for complex functions the brain probably constructs networks which link several quite different parts of the brain and that such networks only become functional for those persons who learn to do those things. We create many of the necessary links in the brain as we learn to engage in literate activities. If we do not engage in literate activities we do not create those linked pathways.

The writing process

The exploring of literacy done by preschool children is more obvious in their early attempts to write than in their attempts to read. They explore the making of marks on paper, from scribble to letter-like forms, to some letter shapes (often those found in their own name), to favourite letters and particular words, and then they acquire more letters and more words. As they are exploring the possibilities of writing, they invent shapes and imaginary words. After they enter school, children work quite hard to understand the conventions of the printer's code, the 'rules' of writing, and while they master some of these quite quickly, the time they take to master others (for example, the space concept, or the importance of letter order, or the difference that orientation of letters makes to what they stand for) is surprisingly long. (See Clay, 2010a, 2010b, 2010c.)

Hannah was very interested in print by her fourth birthday. What is particularly interesting are her mother's notes about what Hannah said and did as she constructed her understanding of the process of writing and the process of reading.

> Mummy, I can read the words I can write.
> If I can write 'cat' I can read it.

> Mummy, the more words I can write the more words I can read.
> (Four months later) I can write 'cat' with my mouth (and then she sounded out 'c-a-t' slowly).

Hannah found things in her environment that interested her. In the garage she noticed the number 10, and her immature writing process went into action.

> Mummy, if the zero was a letter it would be an 'o'
> and if you put a cross on that part it would make 'to'.

This kind of thing happened often; for Hannah they were not exceptional remarks. Her mother asked her whether she had shown her preschool teachers how she could write. Hannah replied, 'No, I haven't shown them. They don't expect me to write.'

Preschool children can learn about many visual features of print, can learn how to write some letters, can know how to write some words, can pretend to write notes or letters to family and friends, or can dictate stories they want written for them. They can do all this before they have begun to consider how the words they say may be coded into print, and in particular how the sounds of speech are coded in print. Hannah is getting close to this as she explores print for fun.

It is a challenge to work out when the written code follows clear-cut rules or when patterns of letters are repeated and when, at other times, irregular patterns may be required. It is an added challenge if you have to learn literacy in two different scripts at the same age (such as English and Hebrew, or French and Chinese). Yet four- to six-year-olds do begin to grapple with these complexities if they are given opportunities to learn both literacies in their environment.

Sometimes the preschool writer gives a lot of attention to the visual forms of letters and words. Pim was a Thai child growing up in the United States. Her bilingual parents read her story books in Thai and in English, and she went to an English-language preschool. By the time she was five years two months she read simple things in English quite well and she wrote for her teacher 'BABY I LOVE YOU'. Interestingly she added to the English letters the little circles which are a feature of the Thai script.

Knowing some of the conventions of print, children can bring what they know about letters and words to bear on the writing task. For many years researchers have been exploring how well children can hear the sounds in the words they are trying to read and write because of the need to notice and learn letter-sound relationships. When they begin to notice the sounds in the words they are speaking young children usually seek someone else's help, or they invent symbols, or they use the little alphabet knowledge they have and find sounds in letter names.

So, there are many facets to the writing process, just as there are to the reading process. They are complementary processes.

1   *Writing involves messages expressed in language.* The writer must compose these messages one letter at a time, but the message can be something he might say in everyday speech.

2   *Writing involves visual learning of letter features and letter forms* — and patterns of letters in clusters or in words — and requires the writer to combine this learning with what he knows about the conventions of the printer's code.

3   *Writing also involves the young writer in listening to his own speech* — to find out which sounds he needs to write — and then finding the letters with which to record those sounds.

Children learn to compose messages they want to write. At first it may not be easy for a child to compose orally what he wants to write, or wants a teacher to write for him, and the quality of composition, in telling stories or conveying information, improves as children immerse themselves in the task (Paley, 1981).

There is, however, a time during the early stages of learning to write when the child must put real effort into working out for himself how the composition can be recorded, and what he, as the writer, has to do to get the story down on paper. Both the composition and the scribing aspects of the task can be approached with success by young children.

As the young writer works earnestly to put his messages on paper he is, like the young reader, working up and down the various levels at which we can analyse language — message, sentence, word, letter cluster, or letter-sound. As a reader he may ignore some of the information in print and lean upon the anchor points of the information he knows. In writing, however, there is no other way to write than letter by letter, one after the other; it is an analytical activity which takes words apart. He may omit letters, or use substitutes for the ones in orthodox spelling, but he is forced by the nature of the task to act analytically on print when he is writing.

The teacher of beginning writers provides opportunities and purposes for writing, engages children's interest as active participants, allows the children to initiate what they can, shares the hard bits of the task with individual children and astutely anticipates when help is needed.

One can list many things that must be learned about printed language which are shared by reading and writing. Some of these are:

• moving in a left to right direction (for English) and controlling serial order

• drawing on language information stored in memory

• making and recognising visual symbols

- using visual and sound information together

- holding the message so far in mind

- drawing on the known words and structures of language

- searching, checking and correcting

and managing to bring these different activities together as a message is constructed.

The young writer explores and extends his letter knowledge and the small set of words he knows, and tries out one or two sentence structures. A breakthrough occurs when, secure in some of these activities, the young writer begins to draw into his writing the flexibility with which he expresses himself orally. So writing involves language but also visual information, sound sequence information, word knowledge, composing, and motor control over the production of symbols and sequences. It is sometimes necessary to lower the demands on form and neatness and correctness of letter formation and text layout for a time, in order to achieve a shift to flexible expression of ideas.

The blank page

Teachers and parents are apt to judge that lines on paper help children. They expect them to produce better products more quickly if given lines.

A different analysis runs like this. Some children, faced with the tasks of learning about print and how to read and write, find motor control difficult. Writing within lines forces children to carry out difficult motions of the hands and eyes. If that constraint costs them too much effort, making it harder to attend to the message they wanted to write, they are likely to avoid writing and turn their attention to something easier. Speaking and reading and thinking and writing can be learned by a child with slow or poor motor coordination but the hand's control over movement is not easily trained, changed or coerced. One has to wait for the coordination to become possible. For the children who find motor tasks difficult it is desirable to press on with the learning of literacy in spite of the poor coordination.

So we can offer the children opportunities to write but in the very early stages we can avoid some demands — we need not be too fussy about print size, keeping to straight lines, making it look good, and expecting the child to know already about directional rules, page layout, and punctuation. There is plenty of scope in daily writing, with a helpful teacher available, for beginning writers to learn new features and conform more and more to conventional expectations. Teachers do not give up their expectations for well-formed writing, but they are more patient and less demanding about the forms of the writing and they focus their teaching on the literacy knowledge to be taken aboard despite any coordination difficulties.

A blank page, used for the two Observation Survey writing assessments, allows the greatest scope to those who have the least control over the writing process. And it should be remembered that the tasks described in this book are not teaching activities; they are opportunities for the child to reveal what he knows and can do.

Seeing print from two vantage points

Most people find it difficult to think of writing and reading as two different ways of learning about the same thing — written language. It is like having two hands. (If you have ever had one hand out of action you will understand this metaphor.) What you know in writing can be helpful in your reading and vice versa, just as the right hand can help the left hand with holding or vice versa. Another analogy that comes to mind is the advantage the automobile driver gains from the side and rear vision mirrors; he or she needs to drive forward but getting extra information about the situation from a different source can be a real help.

A colleague of mine has collapsed three important characteristics of print into an easily remembered mnemonic, DOS (Phillips, 2001). A written language must be read in a certain direction (D), symbols or letters have particular orientations (O), and the rules for laying out the language information in print mean that you must attend to things in a particular sequence (S). The challenges are easily remembered with the mnemonic DOS, but there are many children who have a lot to learn in these three areas.

Independent learners

In summary, teachers aim to produce independent learners whose reading and writing improves whenever they read and write. Children become independent:

- if the early behaviours are appropriate, secure and habituated

- if they learn to *monitor* their own reading and writing

- if they *search* for several kinds of information, in word sequences, in longer stretches of meaning, and in letter sequences

- if they *discover* new things for themselves

- if they *check* that one kind of information fits with other available information

- if they *repeat* themselves as if to confirm what they have read or written

- if they *correct* themselves, taking the initiative for making any sources of information they have found fit neatly together (that is, getting words right)

- and if they *solve* new words by these means.

Each statement above could be applied to either reading or writing.

3 Assisting young children making slow progress

Since I began teaching children to read many years ago the teaching problems have remained much the same, although the services offered have increased and improved and the percentage of children needing special help may have been reduced. Today we have teachers, parents and communities with an awareness of the importance of early literacy learning that did not exist in the 1950s when we were trying to create it.

With the development of community interest there has been a proliferation of naive ideas about what reading is and what reading difficulties are. Incorrect and misleading ideas are often found in the media. Critics of schools sometimes imply that people have different levels of intelligence but that all people can reach a *similar* level in reading achievement. These two expectations are contradictory. Completely erroneous statements are made about words 'seen in reverse' or 'the brain scrambling the signals going to the eyes' or 'squares that look like triangles'. There is no evidence to support such descriptions of how our brain works during reading.

These errors of understanding arise from adults who make superficial or poor observations of their own skills or who disseminate misguided interpretations of new concepts which are only partly understood. Fortunately, this does not have to be the case any longer. Since the 1980s, with new understandings and new practices, we have seen the development of more effective solutions in the area of early interventions and have reached a point where it is possible to hypothesise that all but a very small number of children can learn to read and write and schools are able to implement interventions which can bring this about. Let me give an example:

Livia's preschool experiences were very different when compared with most children. He was over seven years before he was able to start reading books. In his fourth year at school he was reading well at the level of children in their third year at school. In one sense he did not have a reading problem. Once he began to read, his rate of progress was about average. Livia needed reading material and instruction at his level so that he could continue to learn to read and it is only in that sense that he had a reading problem. If he were given harder materials to read, he would work at frustration level and could even 'go backwards' because he would no longer be practising in smooth combination the skills he had developed so far. Striving to work beyond his reading level he could become less and less competent in comparison with his peers because his instruction was not appropriately adapted to his learning needs.

Progress has more to do with engagement in large quantities of successful reading than with exercises in decoding texts which are hard to read. Teachers and the education system should make every effort to reduce the number of children falling below their class level in reading, and public opinion must be kept informed so that non-teachers are able to ask appropriate evaluation questions.

In the past, a teacher of children in their fourth year of school could expect a range of reading achievement in her classroom that spread across five or six years. Among her eight- to nine-year-old children there would be able children who read like young high school students and other children reading like children in the first year of school. The highest achievements come about in part because once a certain command of reading is attained, reading improves every time one reads. There will always be a range of reading achievement for which the class teacher must provide.

Good literacy programmes

Now schools plan to have all children master the fundamentals of literacy learning by about the age of nine years so that almost every child will be able to read and write at levels expected of his or her age group. One way in which the range of achievement could be narrowed would be by lifting the competence of the children in the lower third of the achievement range. This has come to be very important.

If, after that, all children at every point in the new range of normal variation are increasing their level of achievement (even though that achievement will still vary widely because of the high achievers) then the school will be doing its job well. However, all children will still not be able to read in the same way or at the same level any more than they can all think alike. And the complexities of the language will leave teachers with a full curriculum of things to which their students must be introduced.

The first requirement of a good literacy programme is that all teachers check the provisions that they make for the lowest groups in their classes. Is the programme really catering for the full range of literacy knowledge in this class of children? *For learning to occur it is very important to ensure that the difficulty level of the reading material presents challenges from which the child can learn and not difficulties that disorganise what he already knows.* If children in low groups are not reading for meaning, if what they read does not sound like meaningful language, if they are stuttering over sounds or words with no basis for problem-solving the text, they should be taken back to a level of reading and writing tasks where they can orchestrate all the reading processes into a smoothly functioning message-getting process, and all the writing processes into a smoothly functioning message-construction process. (They will read fairly accurately with about one error in ten words and write sentences they have composed for themselves.)

Each classroom needs a wide range of reading books to cater for the expected range of reading skills. All children need both easy and challenging books from which they learn different things. Just as you might find it relaxing on holiday to pick up a light novel, an Agatha Christie or a science fiction book, competent readers enjoy easy reading too. On easy material they practise the skills they have and build up fluency.

Perhaps one or two children in the lowest group do not seem to be able to read anything. It may be that they have been forced to read at frustration level for as long as a year or two, and they may even have lost touch with some of their initial reading competencies. Children can go backwards later in their schooling too, not reading as well as they did at an earlier age. The patterns of progress can be so different that such children may need individual teaching if they are to develop as independent readers of new books.

A useful rule of thumb is to accept that skilful readers and writers can work well on their own if a teacher is available to do a little explaining, and teaching at critical points when they encounter a difficulty. But as we go further down a scale of reading ability students will need more and more of the teacher's time to pull together all that they need to know to read well, and to apply it when necessary to their problem-solving. The poorer the reader the more individual teaching time that learner will require. Writers will need regular and frequent opportunities to write with ready access to a teacher's help.

In a teacher's lowest reading groups there could be one or more children who have had remedial lessons two and three times a week for several years yet have not caught up to their peers. They may improve in reading skills but do not usually make up for those years of learning at a very slow rate and the associated sense of failure. They missed the opportunity to receive early intervention in literacy tutoring during the first years of school. Often this missed opportunity is blamed on the child, their attitude, ability or attendance. More probably, in the majority of cases, schools did not arrange for early intervention to be available to the child.

What are the ingredients of a good reading and writing programme for children of low achievement in classroom settings? For a good programme you need a very experienced teacher who has been trained to think incisively about the reading and writing process and who is sensitive to individual differences; a teacher who has continued to seek professional development and understands the literacy issues of the day, and the particular programme the school is delivering. You need a school which organises for class teachers to give individual attention to the children who have made the least progress, especially in the first two years of school. The teacher carefully sequences the tasks and materials to be read to meet the learning needs of each pupil, and she helps and supports the pupil to read and write successfully most of the time.

A self-extending system

The teacher aims to produce in the pupil a set of behaviours which will ensure a self-extending system. What does that mean? As children move up a gradient of difficulty in texts they develop ways of extending their own competencies so that the more they read or write, the better they get at reading harder texts of increasingly diverse types. The teacher lifts the motivation and challenge and designs rich opportunities for students to explore increasingly complex texts, but the reader or writer begins to shape his own progress. The teacher expects to end up with pupils who are as widely distributed in reading and writing achievement as they are in the population in intelligence, mathematical achievement, sporting skills or cooking prowess. But each pupil should be making progress from where he is to somewhere else.

Frequently, someone approaches me with this kind of statement: 'I'm not a teacher but I would like to help children with reading difficulties. Do you think I could?' My answer is that the best person to help a child with reading difficulties is a trained teacher who has become a master teacher of literacy and who has been trained as a specialist in developing readers and writers with self-extending systems. There are a few ways for para-professionals to work with children with literacy difficulties; that is to listen to them reading many little books or texts that they can read easily, to encourage and motivate them to read and write more, to prompt and help them with a new word or two, and to read harder material to them and write the hard-to-spell parts of their writing.

An expert teacher is needed to expose the child to attempting the harder tasks which challenge the learner to lift his competency to work well on higher level texts, and to teach the child how to develop a self-extending system that will, in time, take over the role of expanding current competencies. Unlike many human conditions, failure to read and write almost never ends in spontaneous recovery.

Early intervention

What we understand about how we learn to read and about the reading process itself has changed as a result of many reports and from intensive research efforts. While the techniques recommended by the older research scholars still have validity (for example, Fernald, 1943), their understanding of the reading process is dated. Theorists now look upon the reading process in a different way and that makes many of the older texts on reading less useful today. It is not enough to work with old concepts and cures to solve reading difficulties. We now have very good reasons for discarding some old concepts that led to ineffective teaching.

If I believed for example that visual images of words had to be implanted by repetition in children's minds, and that a child had to know every set of letter-sound relationships that occur in English words before he could progress in reading books, then I could not explain some of my successes as a teacher. I could not explain how an 11-year-old with a reading age of eight years could make three years' progress in reading in six months, having two short lessons each week. It just would not be possible. A good theory ought at least to be able to explain its successes.

When I surveyed research reports which measured children's reading before remedial work, after their programmes, and then after a follow-up period, the results were almost always the same. Progress was made while the teacher taught, but little progress occurred back in the classroom once the clinical programmes had finished (Aman and Singh, 1983). The children usually did not continue to progress without the remedial teacher. They were not learning reading the way that successful readers learn. Successful readers learn a system of behaviours which continues to accumulate skills merely because it operates. (Exceptional reading clinicians do help children to build self-extending systems but they do not seem to do this frequently enough to influence the research findings.)

In the past we operated with a concept of remedial tuition that worked but did not work well enough. There were clinicians, principals, teachers, and willing folk in the community working earnestly and with commitment. Individual children received help but the size of the problem had not been reduced. Some children were recovered, others were maintained with some improvement and some continued to fail.

Why was this so? Lack of early identification was one reason. In other areas of special education we practised early identification. Deaf babies, our blind and cerebral-palsied preschoolers and others with special needs got special help to minimise the consequential aspects of their handicaps. Yet a child with reading difficulties had to wait until the third or fourth year of school before being offered special instruction. By then the child's reading level was two years behind that of his peers. The learning difficulties of the child might have been more easily overcome if he had practised error behaviour less often, if he had less to unlearn and relearn, and if he still had reasonable confidence in his own ability. Schools must change their organisation to solve these problems early. It takes a child with even the most supportive teacher only three to four months at school to define himself as 'no good at that' when the timetable comes around to reading or writing activities.

Teachers and parents of 11- to 16-year-olds often believe that schools have done nothing for the reading or writing difficulties of the young people they are concerned about. Yet the older child has probably been the focus of a whole sequence of well-intentioned efforts to help, each of which has done little for the child. This does not mean that children do not sometimes succeed with a brilliant teacher, a fantastic teacher-child relationship, or a hardworking parent-child team. What it does mean is that the efforts often fail for want of expert training of the teacher, and for want of persistence and continuity of efforts. They often fail because those efforts are begun too late.

It seemed to me that the longer we left the child failing the harder the problem became and three years was too long. The results of waiting are these.

- There is a great gap or deficit to be made up.

- There are consequential deficits in other aspects of education.

- There are consequences for the child's personality and confidence.

- An even greater problem is that the child has tried to do his work, has practised his primitive skills and has tried to combine his skills in ways that are not effective; the prior learning stands like a block wall between the remedial teacher and the responses that she is trying to get established.

Any remedial programme delivered later in the child's career will have to spend much time helping the pupil to unlearn many of his ways of working. Why have we tended to wait until the child was eight or more years old before offering special assistance?

- We believed, erroneously, that children mature into reading.

- We did not like to pressure children, and we gave them time to settle.

- We knew children who were 'late bloomers' (or we thought we did).

- Our tests were not reliable until our programmes were well under way and we were hesitant to label children wrongly or to use scarce remedial resources on children who would recover spontaneously.

- We did not understand the reading and writing process well enough.

- We thought a change of method, or searching for the magic solution, would one day make the reading problem disappear.

- We believed in simple single causes such as 'not having learned his alphabet or letter-sound relationships'.

- Teachers found it difficult to identify which children were having trouble at the end of the first year of instruction, and often believed that there were no such children in their schools.

- A child has traditionally been considered worthy of special help only if his achievement falls more than two years below the average for his class or age group. That criterion had more to do with the reliability of our achievement test instruments than with any particular learning needs of the children.

In 1962 when I began my research I asked the simple question 'Can we see that something in the reading process is awry in the first year of instruction?' It was, in terms of our techniques at the time, an absurd question. The answer is, however, that today this can be observed by the well-trained teacher. And it is much simpler than administering batteries of psychological tests or trying to interpret the implications of neurological examinations with respect to the activity of reading.

At the end of the first year at school (and also at the end of a preparatory year for five-year-olds) teachers can locate children who seem to need extra help and resources to learn some basic skills and concepts and to unlearn unwanted behaviours, or to put together isolated behaviours into a workable system.

Simple observation tasks like those in the Observation Survey will predict well which young children who have been in instruction for one year have become readers and writers 'at risk'. The children's performance on the tasks also gives the teacher some idea of what to teach next. The second year at school can then be used as a time to catch up with the average group of readers and writers in classrooms.

The sensitive observation of literacy behaviour

The first steps to prevent literacy learning difficulties can be taken in any school system. Sensitive observation of what school entrants can do and careful observation at frequent intervals of children's responsiveness to a good school programme can reveal many individual differences. Researchers are still trying to develop tests which will predict that children are likely to have difficulty, but all such tests must, of necessity, be prone to error because they try to estimate how well a child will perform in an activity he has not even had the opportunity to explore.

Instead of using tests to predict ahead of time something the child has not yet encountered, researchers can use systematic observation of what children are doing as they perform literacy-related tasks in new entrant classrooms. Observation of children's behaviour is a sound basis for the early evaluation of literacy progress. Children may stray off into poor procedures at many points during the first year of instruction.

I refer here to a controlled form of observation which requires systematic, objective recording of exactly what a child does on a particular (sometimes contrived) task. It must be carried out without any accompanying teaching or teacher guidance. This contrasts with several less effective practices — observation while teaching, casual or subjective observation, or judgemental conclusions based on remembered events from fleeting observations while teaching a group of children.

A flexible programme which respects individuality at first, can bring children gradually to the point where group instruction can be provided for those with common learning needs. In schools which have new entrant or reception classes this is one of the main roles of their teachers.

While sensitive observation during the first year is the responsibility of the class teacher, a survey of reading and writing progress after one year of instruction should be undertaken by the school team of teachers to catch any child beginning to stray from a quality path of progress. Many education authorities want to carry out school entry assessment and this might guide the first year of instruction but, if time and resources are short, ***the most critical time in the life of a reader or writer is a year after instruction has begun.*** This survey is held to be desirable and practical, in addition to the observations made by class teachers.

Of 100 children studied in one Auckland-based study (Clay, 1966, 1982), there were children making slow progress because of poor language development whose real problem lay in their inability to form and repeat phrases and sentences. There were many children who wavered for months trying to establish a consistent directional approach to print. There were children who could not hear the separation of words within a spoken sentence, nor the sequence of sounds that occur in words. Some children attended only to the final sounds in words. Two left-handed writers had some persisting problems with direction, but so did several right-handed children. For some children with poor motor coordination the matching of words and spaces with speech was a very difficult task. But other children with fast speech and mature language could not achieve success either, because they could not slow down their speech to their hand speed. They needed help with coordinating their visual perception of print and their fast speech. There were unhappy children who were reticent about speaking or writing, and there were rebellious and resistant children. There were children of low intelligence who made slow progress with enthusiasm, and there were others with high intelligence who worked diligently and yet were seldom accurate. There were those who lost heart when promoted because they felt they were not able to cope, and others who lost heart because they were kept behind in a lower reading group.

A year at school will have given all children a chance to settle, to begin to engage with the literacy programme, to try several different approaches, to be forming good or bad habits. It will not be hurrying children unduly to take stock of their style of progress a year after society introduces them to formal instruction. Indeed, special programmes must then be made available for those children who have been unable to learn from the standard teaching practices. This makes good psychological and administrative sense.

The timing of such a systematic survey will depend upon the policies of the education system regarding:

- entry to school
- promotion and/or retention.

In New Zealand continuous entry on children's fifth birthdays is usually followed by fixed annual promotion at the third-year class level. This allows a flexible time allocation of 18 to 36 months for a child to complete the first two class levels according to an individual child's needs. A slow child who takes a year to settle into the strange environment of school may need extra help in the second year to make average progress before promotion to a third-year class.

A different scenario would occur with fixed age of entry. Children entering school at one time (four-and-a-half to five-and-a-half, or five-and-a-half to six-and-a-half) would be surveyed within or after their first year at school. My preference would be for them to receive individual help at the beginning of the second year, having been promoted rather than retained. An alternative would be to get help to them after six months of the first year, on the assumption that they could be promoted to the second-year class rather than retained. This latter procedure may identify for help children who would 'take off' without help in the second six months of that first year of school.

In school systems where entry occurs at younger ages more relaxed and less urgent policies can be adopted. In systems where entry age levels tend to be higher, formal instruction tends to proceed with more urgency and waiting for a year before identifying children may not be seen as appropriate. The key point to bear in mind is that children must not be left practising inappropriate procedures for too long. On the other hand they cannot be pressured or hurried into learning the fundamental complexities of reading and writing. This leads us back to the child who is having difficulty with school learning towards the end of his first year at school.

Each child still having difficulty after all the appropriate school-level adjustments have been made, will have different things he can and cannot do. Each will differ from others in what is confusing, in what gaps there are in knowledge, in ways of operating on print. The child making very slow progress might respond to an intervention especially tailored to his needs in one-to-one instruction; and well-designed individual instruction can provide a very fast route to performing well alongside peers.

The early detection of literacy learning difficulties

Traditionally, literacy difficulties have been assessed with readiness tests, intelligence tests, and tests of related skills such as language abilities, visual discrimination, phonemic awareness or spelling. These have been used to predict areas which might account for a child's reading failure. The problem with the intricate profiles that such tests produce is that, while they may sketch some strengths and weaknesses in the child's behaviour repertoire, they do not provide much guidance as to what the teacher should try to teach the child during reading activities. The child with limited language skills must still be taught to read, although some authorities advise teachers to wait until the child can speak well. The child with visual perception difficulties can be put on a programme of drawing shapes and finding paths through mazes and puzzles, but he must still be taught to read.

Many research studies have found no benefit resulting from training programmes derived directly from such test results. Training non-readers on pictures or geometric shapes did not produce the necessary gains in reading skill; and oral language training was no more useful. This may well be because the children were learning to analyse data which they were unable to relate to their reading tasks. Again and again research points to the egocentric, rigid and inflexible viewpoint of the younger, slower reader. And yet statements on remediation just as often recommend training the child on 'simpler' materials — pictures, shapes, letters, sounds — all of which require a large amount of skill to transfer to the total situation of reading a message which is expressed in sentence form!

To try to train children to read on pictures and shapes or even on puzzles seems a devious route to reading. One would not deny that many children need a wide range of supplementary activities to compensate for restricted preschool lives; but it is foolish to prepare for reading by painting with large brushes, doing jigsaw puzzles, arranging large building blocks, or writing numbers. Entry to reading can be done more directly with written language (Clay 2010, a, b, c).

Having established that printed text is the remedial medium, one can then allow that simplification, right down to the parts of the letters, may at times be required for some children. However, the larger the chunks of printed language the child can work with, the more quickly he learns and the richer the network of personal experience he can bring to the learning task. We should only dwell on detail long enough for the child to discover its existence, and encourage its use in isolation only when that is essential for completing this task or for further learning.

As a reader the child will use detail within and as a part of the network of information lying in a stretch of print. The relationships of details to patterns in reading have often been destroyed by our methods of instruction. It is so easy for us as teachers and superb readers, or for the designers of reading materials, to achieve that destruction.

There have been many attempts to match teaching methods to the strengths of groups of children. The child with good visual perception is said to benefit from sight-word methods; the child with good phonemic awareness (previously assessed as auditory perception) is thought to make better progress on phonological methods. One author writes, 'Children are physiologically oriented to visual or auditory learning.' Another says, 'Teaching phonics as a relatively "pure" form will place a child at a disadvantage if he is delayed in auditory perceptual ability'! An emphasis on letter formation in writing can direct the learner's attention to the fingers and eyes and *away* from hearing language. Instruction which emphasises one information source as paramount over all others places all children at a severe disadvantage; they would have to learn by themselves many skills that their teachers were not teaching, if they were to become successful readers.

Such matching attempts are simplistic, for English is a complex linguistic system. The way to use a child's strengths and improve his weaknesses is not to specialise in one aspect or another but to design the tasks so that he practises the weakness with the aid of his strong abilities. Rather than take sides on reading methods which deal either with sounds that are synthesised or with sentences which are analysed, it is appropriate to select reading texts with the next three points in mind.

- The text must be easy enough for the learner to bring his existing competencies to the current task.

- Any and every text will contain phonemic richness.

- The semantic and syntactic richness of the text will allow the learner to bring his speaking abilities to the synthesis and analysis of what he is reading.

Close observation of a child's weaknesses will be needed because he will depend on the teacher to structure the task in simple steps to avoid the accumulation of confusions. For one child the structuring may be in the visual perception area. For another it may be in sentence patterns. For a third it may be in the discrimination of sound sequences. For a fourth it may be in directional learning. *It is most likely to be in the bringing together of all these ways of responding, as the reader works sequentially through a text.*

It therefore seems appropriate to seek diagnosis of those aspects of the reading and writing process which are weak in a particular child soon after he has entered instruction. The Observation Survey has been used to provide such information for children taught in very different programmes for beginning reading and writing (in New Zealand, Canada, the United Kingdom, Australia and the United States). The Observation Survey provides a framework within which early reading and writing behaviour can be explored irrespective of the method of instruction. What will vary will be the typical scores on the tasks of the survey after a fixed time in instruction. Children in different programmes of instruction do not score in similar ways.[*]

In what follows there is only slight emphasis on scores and the quantifying of progress. The real value of the tasks in the Observation Survey is to uncover what a particular child controls and what operations (see page 34) and items he could be taught next.

Reading instruction often focuses on items of knowledge — words, letters and sounds. Most children respond to this teaching in active ways. They search for links between the items and they relate new discoveries to old knowledge. They operate on print as Piaget's children operated on problems, searching for relationships which order the complexity of print and therefore simplify it.

---

[*] Stanine tables showing norms drawn from differing school programmes of instruction: New Zealand, Canada, the United Kingdom and the United States, are on pages 151–160.

A kind of end-point of early instruction has been reached when children have *a self-extending system of literacy behaviours* which means that they learn more about reading and writing every time they read and write, independent of instruction. When they read texts of appropriate difficulty for their present skills, using their knowledge of oral and written language and their knowledge of the world, they use a set of operations or strategic activities 'in their heads' which are just adequate for reading or writing the more difficult bits of the text. In the process they engage in problem-solving, a deliberate effort to solve new problems using familiar information and procedures. They notice new things about words, and constructively link these things to what they know about the world around them, and/or about printed language in simple books. Their processing is progressive and accumulative. The newly noticed feature of print, worked upon today, becomes the reference point for another encounter in a few days. 'Television' as a new word becomes a reference point for 'telephone' in a subsequent text. Children are working on two theories: their theory of the world and what will make sense, and a second theory of how written language is created. They are testing these two theories and changing them successively as they read more books and write down messages they have composed.

In the Observation Survey an emphasis will be placed on the operations or strategic activities that are used in reading and writing rather than on test scores or on disabilities.

The terms *operations* or *strategic activities* are used for mental activities initiated by the child to problem-solve the puzzle of getting the messages from a text, or putting messages into texts.

1   A child may have the necessary abilities but may not have learned how to use those abilities in reading. He will not make useful moves to solve his own problems. He must learn how to work effectively with the information in print.

2   Or a child may have made insufficient development in one ability area (say, motor coordination) to carry out some new operation (say, use the directional schema for reading English) without special help. *He must learn how to … in spite of …* A special teacher will know how to analyse the task and help him do that learning.

3   Again, a child may have items of knowledge about letters and sounds and words but be unable to relate one to the other, to employ one (say, letters) as a check on the other (say, words), or to get to the messages in print. He is unable to use his knowledge in the service of getting to the messages. He must learn how to check on his own learning, and how to orchestrate different ways of responding to complete a successful message-getting process.

In any of these instances the task for the reading/writing programme is to get the child to learn to use any and all of the processes that are necessary to read texts of a given level of difficulty.

There is an important assumption in this approach. Strategic activities for solving novel features in print (that is, things this reader has not encountered before) are an important part of a reading experience. By solving a novel feature the competent reader not only gets the message but at the same time may extend his capacity to tackle new messages. I have called this a self-extending system; it is what the novice reader is putting together, and what competent readers have achieved when they are about to move into silent reading and massive amounts of recreational reading. Given a knowledge of some items and some strategic awareness of how to work on print, the reader can apply what he knows to similar items. He has a way of working on new items; we do not need to teach him the total inventory of items.

> Using what he knows so far about how print works can lead the reader to the assimilation of new items of knowledge, or it can help the writer to generate new ways of getting to new words. Problem-solving novel features of print is an important part of two self-extending systems: one for reading and one for writing.

An example may help to clarify this important concept. Teachers through the years have taught children the relationship of letters and sounds. They have traditionally shown letters and given children opportunities to associate sounds with those letters. There seemed to be an obvious need to help the child to translate the letters in his book into the sounds of spoken words. And, in some vague way, this also helps the child to use the sounds in his speech to extend his spelling and story writing.

In our studies of children after one year of instruction we found children at risk in reading who could give the sounds of letters but who found it impossible to hear the sound sequences in the words they spoke. They had been taught to go from letters to sounds but they were unable to check whether they were right because they could not hear the sound sequence in the words they spoke. They were unable to find the sounds in their speech and find letters for recording them. Being able to carry out the first operation, letters to sounds, probably leads easily to its inverse for many children but for some of our children at risk being able to go from letter to sound did not lead to going from sound to a letter by which to record that sound.[*]

---

[*] Arising from such observations in the Reading Recovery research and development project in 1976–77 (and the research of Carol Chomsky, Charles Read, D.B. Elkonin, and I.G. Mattingly published in the 1970s) an assessment task assessing phonemic awareness was added to *The Early Detection of Reading Difficulties* (1979, 1985), and *An Observation Survey of Early Literacy Achievement* (1993, 2002), and the teaching of phonemic awareness was built into the writing section of the daily Reading Recovery lesson.

After six months of special tutoring Tony's progress report at the age of 6.3 emphasises not the item gains (in Letter Identification or Reading Vocabulary) but the actions or operations that he can initiate. He can analyse some initial sounds in words, uses language information, has a good locating response, checks on his own attempts and has a high self-correction rate.

- (aged 5.9) has some early concepts about directionality and one-to-one correspondence but his low letter identification score and zero scores on word tests mean that he is not using visual information to check on letters or words.

- (aged 6.0) has made only slight progress in the visual area. In reading text, he relies heavily on language prediction from picture clues and good memory for text. He makes very little use of visual information and therefore cannot use his phonemic awareness to check on his reading. He rarely self-corrects; the two corrections made were on the basis of words he knew well.

- (aged 6.3) now identifies 37/54 letter symbols, has started accumulating a reading and writing vocabulary and can analyse some initial sounds in words. In reading unpatterned text, he uses language information, keeps his place across the letters in a word and words in a text, uses known reading vocabulary with little hesitation, and uses some initial sounds to check on words. He notices and corrects many of his errors.

An approach to literacy learning which emphasises the acquisition of strategic activities to problem-solve novel aspects of print bypasses questions of reading ages. It demands the recording of what the child does when processing texts of specified difficulty; it refers to the strengths and weaknesses of the strategic moves made, and compares these with a model of similar behaviours used by children who make satisfactory progress in reading. It assumes that the learner gradually constructs a network of different processes for working on printed information which at some level becomes a self-extending system by the time that learner is ready to shift to mostly silent reading. It ensures that the learner can continue to learn to read by reading, and to learn to write by writing.

It seems to be possible to lose literacy skills in much the same way that we lose our fluency in a foreign language if we no longer have the opportunity to speak it. Schools must lift literacy competencies to where people will use, retain and continue to expand them in their everyday life activities, when they are reading the paper, notices or instructions, or working on the Internet.

Observation Survey tasks

The reader may wish to refer to Chapter 1, pages 4–13 of *An Observation Survey of Early Literacy Achievement* before reading this section, noting in particular that teachers are recommended to obtain a profile for a child across all tasks. No single task provides a satisfactory assessment of progress in early literacy.

4 Observation task for Concepts About Print

Concepts About Print

With this task we can observe what children have learned about the way we print language. The Concepts About Print task has been redeveloped for use in several languages and in the Hebrew script (Clay, 1989). It taps into what learners have been noticing about the written language around them in their environments.

As preschool children engage with printed messages and books they learn some things about looking through a book in some orderly kind of way. However, there is a great deal more than that to learn about the written code, and this is learned over an extended period of time. There is no way to explain 'a code' to a young child. If one tried to do this one would be likely to confuse children, but a good diet of book-sharing in the preschool years, plus responding to their efforts to find things in print or to write messages to people, will prepare children quite well for what they will be asked to do when they enter school. As a result of highly varied preschool opportunities different children will know different things when they enter school. It is not really a question of how much they know; it is more a matter of what personal experiences they have had with print, what they have noticed and what they have ignored (Clay, 2010b).

It is easy to observe what children already know by using the Concepts About Print observation task, and teachers will be better prepared to advance any child's understanding when they already know what children are attending to. That is what Concepts About Print is designed to reveal — what children are attending to, rightly or wrongly.

Where does one start to attend to print? In what direction does one move? How does one move through a word? These are features of any written message in any language or script, especially when the message is longer than one word. If we are only thinking of single letters or words it is not too difficult, but give a beginning reader just a couple of lines of print and he can become confused! Because some children fall easily into appropriate ways of looking at print, parents and teachers can underestimate how extraordinarily complex it is to understand some of the rules of the written code. It is very easy to pick up strange ways of exploring print that we teachers may not notice but which can become established habits.

> One little girl surprised me when she moved from right to left across a left page and left to right across a right page. The centrefold of the double-page spread was her starting point. And why not?

Another new entrant to Grade 1 tried to respond to her teacher's instruction which was, 'Copy down this message and be sure to start at the margin.' This girl did her best to comply, given her current understanding of writing messages. However because her paper was the wrong way around her margin was on the right!

> ¡Let there be peace on earth
>
> and let it begin with me

Teachers who observe carefully notice that some concepts about print take more than a year to become established. It takes time to learn to respond without error to the two questions 'What is a letter?' and 'What is a word?' Concepts about print are learned gradually as children become readers and writers.

Revealing what children know

Teachers can choose any one of four Concepts About Print (C.A.P.) story booklets as the test booklet to discover what children already know about print, and what has yet to be learned. This is a task which allows teachers, quite reliably, to see who needs what kind of help.

It shows a teacher which of the children need more teacher attention. *Some* may need some intensive opportunities to learn what many other children at school entry already know. However, in the first two years at school children will often encounter new and unfamiliar ways of putting messages into print. It takes a little time to become accustomed to the consistent and invariant things about print.

On entry to school

When the New Zealand Ministry of Education developed a School Entry Assessment called S.E.A. (1997) they included a Tell Me test of oral language, a maths test called Checkout involving buying things from a shop, and, as a measure of literacy knowledge, they chose the Concepts About Print task. By December 2000 nearly 30,000 result sheets had been returned to the Ministry and were entered in the database. These data were obtained from a self-selected sample of schools because the participating schools had chosen to respond to a request from the Ministry to send in their results.

Children were assessed when they had been at school for about six weeks. The graph on the next page provides evidence that at the beginning of formal literacy instruction these students were spread throughout the whole range of scores on the Concepts About Print task. A small number of children knew all the necessary concepts for learning to read English. Within the next two years every child would need to move towards perfect scoring.

Distribution of Concepts About Print scores of five-year-old school entrants

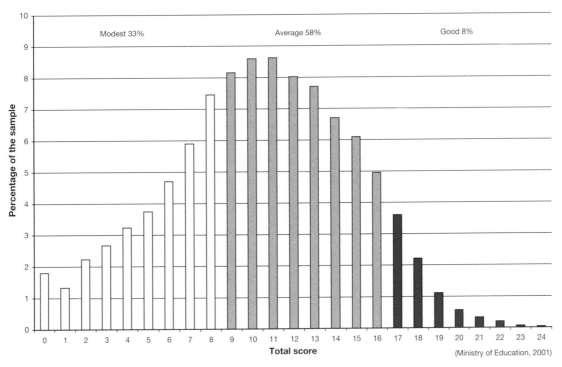

(Ministry of Education, 2001)

Research with children over several decades since 1960 has shown that what is known about letters, sounds and words begins to expand rapidly once children begin literacy activities in school. Concepts must be learned and the teacher's twin goals are first to help children become aware of how print works, and then always to take those concepts into account but to do this without having to pay much attention to them. Conventions that must be accepted are directional movement across print, the orientation of letters (which is not optional), and attending to the sequence of letters or words or ideas (see page 22). A successful learner comes very quickly to act within those rules and rarely has to think about them. Theorists, however, have given too little attention to children who find it particularly challenging to learn how to act within these essential features of a written language code.

How much do children need to know about print?

Eventually children need to follow all the rules but they do not learn them all at once. This learning will come mostly from the opportunities they have to read and write at school. It is a good idea to discover what children already know about books and print because there can be large individual differences in what they can attend to. The differences are not just in how much they know, but also in the fact that one child will understand some aspects of reading and writing which are quite different from the things another child has learned to pay attention to. Teachers must become interested in the differences.

Of course the understanding of some of these arbitrary rules for setting down language in a written form, these printing conventions, is only one aspect of literacy learning: other aspects of literacy learning can be observed with different observation tasks, discussed in Chapters 5–9. The learner needs more than one key to unlock the code. The tasks in *An Observation Survey of Early Literacy Achievement* provide teachers with ways to observe several different aspects of children's literacy learning. When a child understands what to attend to, in what order, and a few things about the shapes and positions of letters and words, this opens other doors to literacy learning.

Reading to the children

In the Concepts About Print observation task the teacher appears to be merely reading the story in the task booklet to the child but she is also asking the child to help. On each page she asks a question or two.

She finds out what the child knows about print: the front of a book, that print (not the picture) tells the story, that there are letters, and clusters of letters called words, that there are first letters and last letters in words, that you can choose upper and lower case letters, that spaces are there for a reason, and that different punctuation marks signal meanings (full stops or periods, question marks, commas, exclamation marks and speech marks).

When we name such things or try to explain some of them to children we must not assume that our verbal explanations have taught children to use their eyes to locate, recognise or otherwise make use of such information. These concepts are learned gradually in reading and writing activities over the first two years of formal schooling.

The four special booklets which have been prepared for this observation task are entitled *Sand* (1972c), *Stones* (1979b), *Follow Me, Moon* (2000c) and *No Shoes* (2000d). They can be used with non-readers or beginning readers; before beginning school or after a time in instruction. The child is asked to help the observer by pointing to certain features of the text *while the observer reads the story*. Five-year-old children have some fun and little difficulty with these tasks. They are not expected to get high scores; the teacher is finding out what is known and what is not known. However, the task remains a sound measuring instrument for most children during the first two years of school.

Observing progress

Children do not need to be able to talk about these concepts. As long as they can learn to work within the directional constraints of print and pay them very little attention they have what is needed to underpin subsequent progress. Confusions with these arbitrary conventions of a written language code can persist among problem readers and interfere with other aspects of literacy learning.

The Concepts About Print task has proved to be a sensitive indicator of behaviours which support reading and writing acquisition, but the test score cannot be expected to stand alone as a prediction device or an indicator of readiness. The concepts are just things the child must come to understand. Becoming involved with literacy activities will help them to grasp some, and eventually all, of these necessary concepts. Sooner is better than later; and it would be absurd to try to build learning activities to teach such concepts before a child is engaged in some kind of reading and writing experiences — these things go hand in hand.

Using the Concepts About Print observation task

Administration

Before starting, become very familiar with the Concepts About Print story that you intend to use, the score sheet and the administration instructions. Giving this assessment in a valid way requires prior practice. Despite the questions which ask for the child's help, the story must be read with sufficient continuity and vitality for the child to be able to gain its meaning and a sense of the flow. Try to avoid adding extra comments.

Develop a standard way of using this observation task, always reading from the administration guide, following the instructions with precision, and making sure that the child understands what he is being asked to do. Position the sheet with the instructions to the side away from the child. After the first item has been given, the book (*Follow Me, Moon*, or *No Shoes*, or *Sand* or *Stones*) should be placed between you and the child so that you can both see it easily.

Administer the items as directed. The administration instructions for giving this task are on pages 44–45. You will need a copy of the Concepts About Print Score Sheet on page 46 for every child. To keep the scoring unobtrusive, you may want to mark incomplete or incorrect responses with a dot. Note down any behaviour under comments.

Read the instructions to the child, as they are written, for each item. Use the *exact* wording given in each demonstration. Move deliberately and demonstrate clearly.

Make sure the child is attending to the print before asking item 10. On items 10, 12, 13 and 14 the observer's position and movements must ensure that the child is attending to the print. If the child does not respond appropriately to item 10, administer item 11, and then you may omit items 12, 13 and 14 (which are likely to be difficult). Read the text on pages 12, 13 and 14 aloud to the child. Continue to administer items 15 to 24 to each child.

Recording and scoring

The instructions for recording and scoring the Concepts About Print task are on pages 44–48.

Say to the child: *'I'm going to read you this story but I want you to help me.'*

COVER

Item 1   Test: For orientation of book.

Pass the book to the child, holding it vertically by outside edge, spine towards the child.

    Say: *'Show me the front of this book.'*
    Score: 1 point for the correct response.

PAGES 2/3

Item 2   Test: Concept that print, not picture, carries the message.
    Say: *'I'll read this story. You help me. Show me where to start reading. Where do I begin to read?'*

Read the text on page 2.

    Score: 1 point for print. 0 for picture.

PAGES 4/5

Item 3   Test: For directional rules.
    Say: *'Show me where to start.'*
    Score: 1 point for top left.

Item 4   Test: Moves left to right on any line.
    Say: *'Which way do I go?'*
    Score: 1 point for left to right.

Item 5   Test: Return sweep.
    Say: *'Where do I go after that?'*
    Score: 1 point for return sweep to left, or for moving down the page.

(Score items 3–5 if all movements are demonstrated in one response.)

Item 6   Test: Word-by-word pointing.
    Say: *'Point to it while I read it.'*

Read the text on page 4 slowly but fluently.

    Score: 1 point for exact matching.

PAGE 6

Item 7   Test: Concept of first and last.

Read the text on page 6. The child must NOT continue word-by-word pointing.

    Say: *'Show me the first part of the story.'*
             'Show me the last part.'
    Score: 1 point if BOTH are correct in any sense, that is, applied to the whole text or to a line, or to a word, or to a letter.

PAGE 7

Item 8   Test: Inversion of picture.
    Say: (slowly and deliberately) *'Show me the bottom of the picture.'*
             (Do NOT mention upside-down.)
    Score: 1 point for verbal explanation, OR for pointing to top of page, OR for turning the book around and pointing appropriately.

PAGES 8/9

Item 9   Test: Response to inverted print.
    Say: *'Where do I begin?'*
             'Which way do I go?'
             'Where do I go after that?'

Read the text on page 8 now.

    Score: 1 point for beginning with 'The' (*Sand*), or 'I' (*Stones*), or 'I' (*Moon*), or 'Leaves' (*Shoes*), and moving right to left across the lower and then the upper line, OR 1 point for turning the book around and moving left to right in the conventional manner.

PAGES 10/11

Item 10   Test: Line sequence.
    Say: *'What's wrong with this?'*

Read immediately the bottom line first, then the top line. Do NOT point.

    Score: 1 point for comment on line order.

PAGES 12/13

Item 11   Test: A left page is read before a right page.
    Say: *'Where do I start reading?'*
    Score: 1 point for indicating the left page.

Item 12   Test: Word sequence.
    Say: *'What's wrong on this page?'* (Point to **page number 12**, NOT the text.)

Read the text on page 12 slowly as if it were correctly printed.

    Score: 1 point for comment on either error.

Item 13   Test: Letter order. (Changes to first or last letters.)
    Say: *'What's wrong on this page?'* (Point to **page number 13**, NOT the text.)

Read the text on page 13 slowly as if it were correctly printed.

    Score: 1 point for any ONE re-ordering of letters that is noticed and explained.

PAGES 14/15

Item 14

Test: Re-ordering of letters within a word.

Say: *'What's wrong with the WRITING on this page?'*

Read the text on page 14 slowly as if it were correctly printed.

Score: 1 point for ONE error noticed.

Item 15

Test: Meaning of a question mark.

Say: *'What's this for?'* (Point to or trace the question mark with a finger or pencil.)

Score: 1 point for explanation of function or name.

PAGES 16/17

Test: Punctuation.

Read the text on page 16.

Say: *'What's this for?'*

Item 16

Point to or trace with a pencil, the full stop (period).

Score: 1 point.

Item 17

Point to or trace with a pencil, the comma.

Score: 1 point.

Item 18

Point to or trace with a pencil, the quotation marks.

Score: 1 point.

Item 19

Test: Capital and lower case letters.

Say: *'Find a little letter like this.'*

Sand: Point to capital T and demonstrate by pointing to an upper case T and a lower case t if the child does not succeed.

Stones: As above for S and s.

Moon: As above for P and p.

Shoes: As above for W and w.

Say: *'Find a little letter like this.'*

Sand: Point to capital M, H in turn.

Stones: Point to capital T, B in turn.

Moon: Point to capital M, I in turn.

Shoes: Point to capital M, I in turn.

Score: *Sand:* 1 point if BOTH m and h are located.

Stones: 1 point if BOTH t and b are located.

Moon: 1 point if BOTH m and i are located.

Shoes: 1 point if BOTH m and i are located.

PAGES 18/19

Item 20

Test: Words that contain the same letters in a different order.

Read the text on page 18.

Say: *'Show me "was".'*
'Show me "no".'

Score: 1 point for BOTH correct.

PAGE 20

Have two pieces of light card (13 cm x 5 cm) that the child can hold and slide easily over the line of text to block out words and letters. To start, lay the cards on the page but leave all print exposed. Open the cards out between each question asked.

Item 21

Test: Letter concepts.

Say: *'This story says:*
Sand: "The waves splashed in the hole".
Stones: "The stone rolled down the hill".
Moon: "The moon followed me home".
Shoes: "My shoes were by the river".
I want you to push the cards across the story like this until all you can see is (deliberately with stress) *JUST ONE LETTER.'* (Demonstrate the movement of the cards but do not do the exercise.)

Speak deliberately. Stress the item.

Say: *'Now show me two letters.'*

Score: 1 point if BOTH are correct.

Item 22

Test: Word concept.

Say: *'Show me just one word.'*
'Now show me two words.'

Score: 1 point if BOTH are correct.

Item 23

Test: First and last letter concepts.

Say: *'Show me the first letter of a word.'*
'Show me the last letter of a word.'

Score: 1 point if BOTH are correct.

Item 24

Test: Capital letter concepts.

Say: *'Show me a capital letter.'*

Score: 1 point if correct.

See page 47 for quick reference to scoring standards for this task.

☐ *Sand*
☐ *Stones*
☐ *Moon*
☐ *Shoes*

CONCEPTS ABOUT PRINT SCORE SHEET

Date: _____

Name: _____ Age: _____ TEST SCORE: [/24]

Recorder: _____ Date of Birth: _____ STANINE GROUP: [ ]

PAGE	SCORE	ITEM	COMMENT
Cover		1. Front of book	
2/3		2. Print contains message	
4/5		3. Where to start	
4/5		4. Which way to go	
4/5		5. Return sweep to left	
4/5		6. Word-by-word matching	
6		7. First and last concept	
7		8. Bottom of picture	
8/9		9. Begins 'The' (*Sand*)	
		Begins 'I' (*Stones*)	
		Begins 'I' (*Moon*)	
		Begins 'Leaves' (*Shoes*)	
		bottom line, then top, OR turns book	
10/11		10. Line order altered	
12/13		11. Left page before right	
12/13		12. One change in word order	
12/13		13. One change in letter order	
14/15		14. One change in letter order	
14/15		15. Meaning of a question mark	
16/17		16. Meaning of full stop (period)	
16/17		17. Meaning of comma	
16/17		18. Meaning of quotation marks	
16/17		19. Locate: m h (*Sand*); t b (*Stones*); m i (*Moon*); m i (*Shoes*)	
18/19		20. Reversible words 'was', 'no'	
20		21. One letter: two letters	
20		22. One word: two words	
20		23. First and last letter of word	
20		24. Capital letter	

Quick reference for scoring standards

Item	Pass standard
1	Front of book.
2	Print (not picture).
3	Points top left at 'I dug ...' (*Sand*) or 'I saw ...' (*Stones*) or 'I said ...' (*Moon*) or 'When I ...' (*Shoes*).
4	Moves finger left to right on any line.
5	Moves finger from the right-hand end of a higher line to the left-hand end of the next lower line, or moves down the page.
6	Word-by-word matching.
7	Both concepts must be correct, but may be demonstrated on the whole text or on a line, word or letter.
8	Verbal explanation, or pointing to top of page, or turning the book around and pointing appropriately.
9	Score for beginning with 'The' (*Sand*) or 'I' (*Stones*) or 'I ran' (*Moon*) or 'Leaves' (*Shoes*) and moving right to left across the lower line and then the upper line, OR turning the book around and moving left to right in the conventional movement pattern.
10	Any explanation which implies that line order is altered.
11	Says or shows that a left page precedes a right page.
12	Notices at least one change of word order.
13	Notices at least one change in letter order.
14	Notices at least one change in letter order.
15	Says 'Question mark', or 'A question', or 'Asks something'.
16	Says 'Full stop', 'Period', 'It tells you when you've said enough' or 'It's the end'.
17	Says 'A little stop', or 'A rest', or 'A comma'.
18	Says 'That's someone talking', 'Talking', 'Speech marks'.
19	Locates two capital and lower case pairs.
20	Points correctly to both 'was' and 'no'.
21	Locates one letter and two letters on request.
22	Locates one word and two words on request.
23	Locates both a first and a last letter.
24	Locates one capital letter.

Mark the child's responses on the Score Sheet as instructed. You can simply total the number of items passed and make a note of what the child knows and what has yet to be learned. Use the Quick Reference for Scoring Standards to guide your decisions as to whether a child's response meets the required criteria.

Stanine scores

To compare the child's performance with that of other children use one of the tables of scores below. In this book each task has four age tables. Select the table which will allow you to compare the child's score with those of other children of his age (see page 126). Look up the total raw score obtained by the child you assessed on the age table that is right for him and read from the second line of boxes his scaled score, a number between 1 and 9.

This scaled score is called a stanine and it provides a guide to how well the child compares with a sample of 796 New Zealand children in February 2000. If the score on the table is allocated across more than one stanine group choose the lowest value: that is, be conservative rather than generous. Read the following section on 'Interpreting Concepts About Print scores' for more information.

CONCEPTS ABOUT PRINT STANINES FOR FOUR AGE GROUPS

Concepts About Print: 5.00 – 5.50 years
(N = 223; Score Range: 0–24; Mean = 13.5; SE = 0.23; SD = 3.5)

Test Score	0–7	8–9	10–11	12–13	14	15–16	17–18	19	20+
Stanine Grp	1	2	3	4	5	6	7	8	9

Concepts About Print: 5.51 – 6.00 years
(N = 170; Score Range: 0–24; Mean = 15.5; SE = 0.28; SD = 3.7)

Test Score	0–8	9–11	12–13	14–15	16–17	18	19–20	21–22	23–24
Stanine Grp	1	2	3	4	5	6	7	8	9

Concepts About Print: 6.01 – 6.50 years
(N = 230; Score Range: 0–24; Mean = 18.0; SE = 0.23; SD = 3.4)

Test Score	0–11	12–14	15–16	17	18–19	20	21–22	23	24
Stanine Grp	1	2	3	4	5	6	7	8	9

Concepts About Print: 6.51 – 7.00 years
(N = 173; Score Range: 0–24; Mean = 18.7; SE = 0.24; SD = 3.2)

Test Score	0–13	14–15	16–17	18	19–20	21	22–23	— 24 —	
Stanine Grp	1	2	3	4	5	6	7	8	9

(For more technical information see Appendices.)

Immediately preceding the summary of the Observation Survey results (Chapter 10, pages 126–128), there is a general discussion of stanine scores, why they are used, when they are helpful and what their limitations are.

You will find national stanines for Canada, the United Kingdom and the United States for each Observation Survey task on pages 155–160.

Interpreting Concepts About Print scores

These concepts about print can be learned in the first years of school. The task's greatest value is the guidance that it gives to teachers. Items uncover concepts yet to be learned or confusions to be untangled. Young children get low scores early in their schooling, and their scores should increase as their reading and writing improves. Teachers should see a control over these concepts gradually emerging, and reassessing at spaced intervals will show that change is occurring in individual children.

Teachers should examine the child's performance carefully and then gradually teach the unknown concepts. ***The items are not in a difficulty sequence because the reading of the story did not allow for this.***

Some indication of difficulty level of particular items for New Zealand children is given in the Age Expectations table (below), which gives the age at which average children passed each item (in a 1972 study). Notice which items children find difficult at first and tend to learn later. What is easy or difficult will be highly dependent on the teaching programme, its activities and emphases, and the expectations held in any particular school.

AGE EXPECTATIONS FOR ITEMS *(Age at which 50 percent of average European children pass an item; Clay, 1972b)*																								
ITEM	1	2	3	4	5	6	7	8	9	10	11	12	13	14	15	16	17	18	19	20	21	22	23	24
Age 5:0		x																						
5:6	x		x	x	x	x	x	x	x	x	x										x			
6:0																			x	x		x		
6:6												x	x		x								x	x
7:0														x		x	x	x						

Most of these Concepts About Print items tell us something about what the children are attending to on the printed page. In items 12 to 14:

- first the words have been placed in the wrong order

- then the letters at the beginning or end of words have been re-ordered

- and finally the letters in the middle of words have been rearranged.

These items focus attention on the importance of attending to print in a left to right sequence. There is a very steep gradient of difficulty on items 12 to 14. Children usually notice the changed word order (item 12) before a change in first and last letters (item 13) or a change in the letters buried within the word (item 14); and many children take a long time to sort out the difference between what people call a word and what people call a letter!

Concepts that children have yet to learn can usually be developed while children are exploring a variety of texts and teachers can focus on particular needs that have been identified (Ministry of Education, 1997). *The problematic thing is that if teachers are not expecting and watching for a gradual change towards control over all these concepts, then some children will be practising many misconceptions or a variety of confusions. When these go unnoticed they can become habituated and hard to change.*

A child's knowledge of Concepts About Print will change over the first years of school, and all children will move towards perfect performance. This is not a prediction device; it yields information for instruction. Confusion is reduced and the runway is cleared for take-off! The main purpose of the scale is to provide teachers with an initial score so that changes in each child's performance can be recorded 6, 12 or 18 months later. To be a successful reader a child must come to control all the concepts tested by this task. Change occurs from (a) having a little knowledge, towards (b) having a control of all these concepts which happens for most children within about two years of beginning literacy learning.

Achia's critique of this task

Achia was being retested on the Concepts About Print task after a period of intensive individual instruction. She asked her teacher if she could write to the author about the story book used in this task. I think she now has a good understanding about the conventions of print.

5 Taking records of reading continuous texts — Running Records

Running Records

This chapter describes some of the key ideas about using Running Records as an assessment of text reading. It introduces how to take and score a reliable record, and how that record can be interpreted. (Relevant discussion of literacy learning theories associated with this approach may be found in Clay, 1991, 1998, 2001, 2005a and 2010b.)

Reading the messages

Running Records provide an assessment of text reading. They are designed to be taken as a child reads orally from any text. The successful early reader brings his speech to bear on the interpretation of print. His vocabulary, sentence patterns and pronunciation of words provide him with information which guides his identification of printed words.

The young reader learns to follow the directional conventions of written language and until he learns something about how his eyes should scan the print, he is unlikely to make much progress with trying to read. Gradually the successful learner begins to move his eyes across the lines and over the page, searching for things he can recognise. He becomes attentive to the visual detail of words, to the spaces, the letters and the sounds that are represented. At the same time he begins to pull more than one kind of information into the 'simple' act of reading. This early phase in learning to read can be understood as laying down several layers of knowledge that are the foundation of subsequent success.

Another view

Typically children's progress in learning to read is measured by testing the number of letters, or sounds, or words they know. Yet most of the time in classrooms they are asked to read continuous texts: they are asked to put together the messages transmitted by the letters, sounds or words.

If Running Records are taken in a systematic way they provide evidence of how well children are learning to direct their knowledge of letters, sounds and words to understanding the messages in the text. The example from a child's reading of text below explains the task. Look at the difficulty of the text. Count the child's errors and self-corrections (SC). Think about the things that challenged this child, the substitutions he made, and what made him correct the last substitution. The record provides evidence of the kinds of things that this child can do with the information he can get from print.

From *The Wolf and the Seven Little Kids* (retold by Fran Hunia, illustrated by Nina Price) in *Horrakapotchkin*.

Reprinted courtesy of Learning Media, Wellington, New Zealand.

Records are taken to guide teaching

Running Records capture what young readers said and did while reading continuous text, usually little short stories. Having taken the record, teachers can review what happened immediately, leading to a teaching decision on the spot, or at a later time as they plan for next lessons. They can judge what the reader already knows, what the reader attended to, and what the reader overlooked. They can assess how well each reader is pulling together what he or she already knows about letters, sounds and words in order to get to the messages. This kind of information allows teachers to prompt, support and challenge individual learners. The records allow teachers to describe how children are working on a text.

Teachers may have to learn some new terms and concepts in order to interpret their Running Records. The procedures are simple, yet what those teachers record can challenge them to think with greater clarity about the progress of beginning readers.

Records are taken to assess text difficulty

One use of a Running Record is as a check on whether students are working on material of appropriate difficulty, neither too difficult nor too easy, but offering a suitable level of challenge to the learner.

Records are taken to capture progress

From the time a child tries to retell a story from the pictures in a book until he has become a silent reader, Running Records, taken at selected intervals, can plot a path of progress. As teachers try to interpret each Running Record, they take into account the difficulty level of the text and make sound judgements about the reader's progress up through a gradient of difficulty in the reading books. A desirable path of progress shows that learners are meeting the challenges of increasingly difficult texts.

The examples in this book are selected to demonstrate how Running Records can be taken on both simple and more advanced texts.

Compare two Running Records on the same text

This is a simple illustration of what a teacher could learn from Running Records. Peter and John read the same text and the records show that they need different emphases in their instruction.

Peter's record

Peter used some visual information from the print and was paying some attention to sentence structure (because his errors usually belonged to a class of words which could occur in the sentence up to the error). He did not react to the lack of meaning in what he said.

John's record

The Bicycle	Accuracy 85.5%		Count		Analysis of Errors and Self-corrections		The Bicycle
Title			E	SC	**Information used**		
					E MSV	SC MSV	The clown got on
✓ ✓ ✓ ✓							and the lady got on
✓ ✓ girl/lady ✓ ✓			I		Ⓜ Ⓢ v		and the boy got on
✓ ✓ man/boy ✓ ✓			I		Ⓜ Ⓢ v		and the girl got on
✓ ✓ ✓ ✓ ✓							and the bear got on
✓ ✓ ✓ ✓ ✓							and the bicycle got . . .
✓ ✓ bike/bicycle ✓			I		Ⓜ Ⓢ Ⓥ		squashed.
flat/squashed			I		Ⓜ Ⓢ v		

John used language information and all his errors reflected the use of meaning and sentence structure. He did not seem to be aware of the mismatch between what he said and the visual information in the text.

These examples show that Running Records can capture how beginning readers are putting together what they know in order to read text. We may question the quality of the text but it did reveal how these two children were working in different ways on the same book.

Learning to take a Running Record

About three workshop training sessions with a teacher who is very familiar with Running Records are recommended for teachers before they begin to use this as an assessment technique. It takes more than self-teaching from a manual to achieve a high standard of observing, recording and interpreting. However, children do some unusual things, so further discussions with colleagues should be scheduled. From time to time school teams should schedule monitoring sessions to review whether the recording and interpretation of Running Records is being conducted with consistency.

In every sense this activity of taking Running Records should be as relaxed as sharing a book with a child. Invite children to read to you and tell them that you will be writing down some things. That gives them a little warning that for the next few minutes you are not going to teach. Those teachers who have practised with a wide variety of children and are at ease in taking Running Records will be the teachers who get the most informative records and will make the fairest interpretations.

What does skilled record-taking look like?

A classroom teacher should, ideally, be able to sit down beside a child with a blank sheet of paper and take a Running Record when the moment is right. Teachers should practise until it is as easy as that. (See pages 80–81 for the many uses of Running Records.) Any text, at any time, as and when appropriate, should be the aim. Then this technique will be flexible enough to suit any classroom conditions. It will also be more likely that the teacher's record can be relied upon to be a 'true account'. (Turn to page 58 for a simple example.)

Teachers should prepare themselves to get the record down while the child is reading. At first, the easy-to-notice things are recorded; with practice it becomes easy to record more. When they can record the essentials, teachers find it easy to note also what the child said about the task, or how they moved across print, or which hand they used to point, and other interesting things like turning back several pages and correcting an earlier error. With practice teachers get more information from their observations and records.

At first, the task seems to require one's whole attention without interruption but before long teachers become bold enough to work in a busy classroom. If a teacher needs to say, at the foot of a page, 'Just a minute; I'm a bit slow today', children will wait. Before long the rest of the class comes to accept that the taking of Running Records is common practice and they will leave the teacher alone to get the job done.

Two things to avoid

Teachers should learn to take Running Records in ways that will allow them to use this technique with standard administration, recording and interpretation.

Printed text: There is not enough room on a pre-printed page of text for the teacher to record all the unusual things that can occur. Many teachers are surprised to find that a printed text often will not allow all of the child's behaviours to be recorded. This is because a Running Record is not just about right or wrong words; it is about a lot more than that. Beginning readers do not keep closely to the text: they sometimes leave out large sections and insert things that are not there; they change direction, go back over what they have read, and confuse themselves.

A Running Record needs to capture all the behaviour that helps us to interpret what the child was probably doing. Everything the child said and did tells us something; when the reading is correct, what his hands and eyes were doing, the comments he made, when he repeated a line of text, and so on. The aim is this: after a Running Record a teacher should be able to 'hear the reading again' when reviewing the record.

Limiting observations to a few select texts pre-printed on a scoring sheet will provide less usable information. Readers do very interesting things as they attempt to get an acceptable message from the pages of a book, and the object of Running Records is to get valid records of how children are arriving at their decisions. Authors and publishers try to 'make it easy' for teachers by providing pre-printed texts but children's problem-solving on texts is too diverse to conform to a published layout. A printed text encourages teachers to attend only to right and wrong responses, and *to ignore how the child is arriving at these decisions.*

Voice recording: Avoid the use of a voice recorder. Having to record the assessment is a crutch to get rid of as soon as possible, so why not start without it. Voice recording may seem easier at first, but it limits the analysis because only sounds and language are recorded. It provides no information about how the child moved, seemed puzzled, peered at the print or looked at the ceiling. Observations like those are helpful for understanding what young learners are trying to do.

Select children who will make practising easier

Practise on a range of readers who are about one year into school, as many as you can. Avoid practising on higher or lower progress readers until you become skilled. Good readers go too fast, and struggling readers produce complex records. For each child make records of two or three little books, or text pieces with about 100–200 words in each, and have the child read each whole story or text. At the early reading level when the child is reading the simplest books, the numbers of words may fall below 100 but if three texts are read this will be satisfactory even though the extracts themselves are short. Once a teacher knows how to take Running Records it should take about 10 minutes to get three samples. Sharing your early records with a teacher who uses them a lot will produce useful discussions.

Select some texts for practising

Any texts can be used for Running Records — books, stories, information texts, or children's published writing — but a good place to start is with a familiar text that the child has read once or twice before. This 'seen' text will provide evidence of how the reader is bringing different processes and skills together. A classroom teacher would probably select something the child has recently read in class. *The prime purpose of a Running Record is to understand more about how children are using what they know to get to the messages of the text, or in other words what reading processes they are using.*

Children who are proficient readers can be assessed for a different purpose — to see how they read a new, unseen text — revealing a *level* of achievement.

It is a good idea to start each assessment with a text that is easy for this child. An 'easy level' book will also be easy for teachers to record as they rehearse their recording techniques.

The teacher may want to know how the child performs on a challenging text. Sometimes the teacher discovers that the child can work at a higher level than that teacher anticipated. A challenging text could show whether the reader recognises the need for problem-solving and what kinds of problem-solving this reader tries. However if the challenges are too great the record will not show how the reading process comes together, only how and when it falls apart.

A text at each of the easy, instructional or hard levels will provide the necessary evidence for a concise summary of where that child is in his learning when administering the Observation Survey. (Record the text level on each Running Record sheet.) The terms easy, instructional and hard used in Running Records do not describe the characteristics of the text itself. ***They describe how a particular child read the text.*** They do not say anything about how another child will read that text. Whether it is easy or instructional or difficult is determined entirely by how well the child was able to work on it. When publishers suggest some order of difficulty in their books they are usually estimating how 'children in general' might find these books. Look for evidence of whether the publishers trialled their books on a sample of children and whether those children were anything like the children you teach.

When a child reads a text at between 90 and 94 percent accuracy level, this is called an instructional level because it indicates an appropriate level for this child to learn from. The record will contain evidence of problem-solving because it will contain some error. Teachers can then observe how children work at monitoring their own reading. In the young reader we can hear and record how the child is problem-solving (also called 'processing the information') but as readers become proficient more of the processing is hidden from view, worked out in the child's head before a response is made.

For important educational decisions it is not enough for teachers to assess children only on their current reading books. Recording their performance at three levels of text difficulty — an easy text (95 to 100 percent correct), an instructional text (90 to 94 percent correct), and a hard text (80 to 89 percent correct) — is a more reliable way to establish what level of text should be used for instruction. ***When a gradient of difficulty in text level is being used, the highest level text the child can read with 90 percent accuracy or above indicates the instructional level***. Research shows that children's learning is helped when we give them material at their personal instructional level. This more careful approach would be used for important educational decisions like:

- moving children to groups for instruction

- observing children with particular difficulties

- selecting children for special and supplementary assistance

- making decisions about promotion

- or for a school survey of achievement.

For research studies three levels of difficulty ***must*** be obtained to ensure that the assessments are reliable.

Older proficient readers become fast readers, too fast for the teacher to make ticks (checks) for every word. Then the observer can give up recording the correct responding, and, keeping strictly to the layout and lines of the text, record all the processing the reader does to monitor, solve words and self-correct. This is a compromise made only for very fast readers. The record needs to be analysed immediately for it is hard to recapture the 'reading' from such a limited record.

How to record what you see and hear

Administration

The next record of a book read well provides an illustration of many but not all of the recording techniques. The record must mimic the layout of lines in the text the child is reading.

Text	Record
"A bee!" said Baby Bear.	✓ ✓ ✓ ✓ ✓
"Where is he going?"	✓ ✓ ✓ ✓
The bee went into a tree.	✓ ✓ ✓ ✓ ✓ bush | R | SC / tree | |
Baby Bear looked in the tree.	✓ ✓ looks | SC ✓ a | R | SC ✓ / looked | the | |
"Honey!" said Baby Bear.	✓ ✓ ✓ ✓
"Honey for me! Thank you, bee."	✓ ✓ ✓ ✓ ✓ ✓

Some observers find that entering the fullstops (periods) helps them to keep track of the recording and scoring.

Text	Record
"Honey!" said Baby Bear.	✓ ✓ ✓ ✓ .
"Honey for me! Thank you, bee."	✓ ✓ ✓ ✓ ✓ ✓ .

However there are problems when teachers try to record pausing and phrasing because teachers' practices then tend to be unreliable.

Standard ways of recording are recommended to take care of almost all the unusual behaviours teachers might encounter. The conventions described have been widely used with children who are reading English. The recording is easy for teachers to use and is also reliable as an assessment. Running Records are not limited to a particular theory of literacy learning. However, in any interpretation of the record, the teacher's theory of literacy learning begins to become involved. (This is discussed on pages 71–75.)

Why use standard procedures?

If a teacher claims that a child read a text with a certain level of accuracy, we need to be assured that this has been obtained according to common practice. If this is not true then calculations and comparisons do not have any meaning. This is a very important statement.

Teachers want to be able to compare Running Records one with another. Either they want to know how John's record today compares with his earlier records, or they need to make some teaching decision about several children and to compare one reader with another. The aim is to take a full record, recording and scoring it reliably so comparisons can be made. To make comparisons, teachers need to have a common standard for taking records, for describing what they observe, for calculating the scores and interpreting the record.

To support the interpretation of the record, teachers should also try to write down the comments children make as they read the book; working out loud, talking to themselves, being surprised, giving some rationale for what they did, and any personal reactions.

Conventions for recording

1   Mark every word read correctly with a tick (or check).

A record of the first five pages of the 'Ready to Read' (1963) book *Early in the Morning* that was 100 percent correct would look like this. (The lines indicate page breaks.)

Bill is asleep.	✓ ✓ ✓
'Wake up, Bill,'	✓ ✓ ✓
said Peter.	✓ ✓
Sally is asleep.	✓ ✓ ✓
'Wake up, Sally,'	✓ ✓ ✓
said Mother.	✓ ✓
Father is shaving.	✓ ✓ ✓

2   Record a wrong response with the text under it.

> *Child:* home
> Text: house   [One error]

3   If a child tries several times to read a word, record all his trials.

> *Child:* here | h— | home
> Text: house | | [One error]

> *Child:* h— | ho— | ✓
> Text: home | | [No error]

Note that in both examples the child was judged to be solving the word, and not correcting an error.

4   If a child succeeds in correcting a previous error this is recorded as 'self-correction' (written SC).

> *Child:* where | when | SC
> Text: were | | [No error]

5   If no response is given to a word it is recorded with a dash. Insertion of a word is recorded over a dash.

> No response   Insertion
>
> *Child:*   —   *Child:*   here
> Text: house   Text: —   [In each case one error]

For contractions see page 67, 11C.

6   If the child baulks, unable to proceed a) because he is aware he has made an error and cannot correct it, or b) because he cannot attempt the next word, he is told the word (written as T). This preserves the storyline and starts the reader off again. (Wait no more than about three seconds.)

> *Child:* home | — |
> Text: house | T house | T   [One error]

7   A verbal appeal for help (A) from the child is turned back to the child for further effort. Say '*You* try it' (recorded as Y). The response from the teacher is *not* a teaching interaction; it involves no prompting but is merely a shift of the initiative.

Child:	—	A		✓	✓	
Text:	house		Y			[One error]

8   Sometimes the child gets into a state of confusion and it is necessary to extricate him. The most detached method of doing this is to say 'Try that again', marking TTA on the record. This would not involve any teaching, but the teacher needs to indicate where the child should begin again. Put square brackets around the first set of muddled behaviour, enter the TTA, remember to count that as one error only (see page 67), and then begin a fresh record of the problem text. An example of this recording would be:

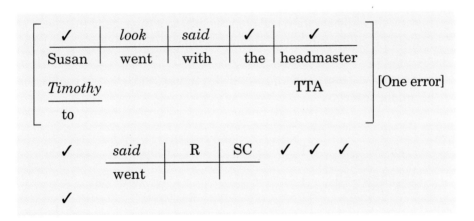

	✓	*look*	*said*	✓		✓	
	Susan	went	with	the	headmaster		
	Timothy				TTA		[One error]
	to						

	✓	*said*	R	SC	✓	✓	✓
		went					
	✓						

9   Repetition (R) is not counted as error behaviour. Sometimes it is used to confirm a previous attempt. Often it results in self-correction. It is useful to record this behaviour as it often indicates how much sorting out the child is doing. R, standing for repetition, is used to indicate repetition of a word, with R_2 or R_3 indicating the number of repetitions. If the child goes back over a group of words, or returns to the beginning of the line or sentence in his repetition, the point to which he returns is shown by an arrow.

Child:	*Here is the home*	R	SC	
Text:	Here is the house			[No error]

10   Sometimes the child rereads the text (repetition) and corrects some but not all errors. The following example shows the recording of this behaviour.

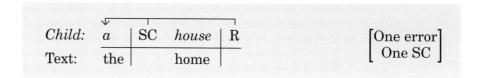

11   If a child spells or sounds out the letters of a word, record capitals for spelling (as in HELP) and record letter or cluster breaks (as in h-e-l-p-ing) for sounding out.

12   Directional attack on the printed text is recorded by telling the child to 'Read it with your finger.' Sometimes you may notice signs that tell you the young reader is not following the directional rules for attending to print. To check on this select a few lines of print during the reading and say to the child, 'Read it with your finger.' A brief observation will often be sufficient but extend the observation if you need to understand more about this behaviour. Even if teachers do not find pointing a desirable teaching prompt, they will still need to use it to collect some evidence of starting points, direction of scanning, and lapses or confusions from beginning readers.

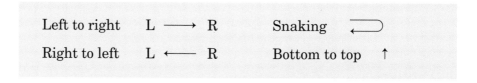

13   As soon as the reading ends, ask yourself, 'How did the reading of that text sound?' Add a comment at the end of the Running Record (see page 63).

14   Other behaviours. The conventions for recording and scoring relate only to correct responses, errors, and self-corrections. Other behaviours include pausing, sounding out the letters, and splitting words into parts. Research evidence has shown that teachers' records of such behaviours are much less reliable and cannot be included in the count or analysis scoring.

A Running Record from a child who is making many errors is hard to record and score but the rule is to record as much of the behaviour as you can, and analyse objectively what is recorded.

How the reading sounds

Describe the reading behaviour recorded: it is important to listen closely to the reading as it occurs, since it provides information about the child's current literacy learning. Immediately following the reading and before you begin to analyse the processing detail of the record, write a few lines on what you just observed, your intuitive summation of the child's reading. This should be an overall reaction. Comment on what the reader did well. Was the reading done at a good pace, or was it slow, or too fast? Was he reading groups of words together in a phrased way? Are things in balance or out of balance in your judgement? Attend particularly to change over previous readings.

Assessment and comprehension

Running Records should be valued because they adhere to good assessment practices. Some teachers wish to add retelling or comprehension questions to the taking of a Running Record. Here are some comments and cautions.

- Comprehension is very dependent upon the difficulty level of the text. It makes no sense to assess comprehension on a hard text, nor on an easy text. If the text level is instructional then that tells the teacher to teach for understanding.

- Because different teachers ask different questions their comprehension questions provide an unreliable gauge of comprehension.

- The answers to comprehension questions depend more upon the difficulty of the sentence structure of the question than on the child's reading, according to research.

The reliability and validity of these assessments are not improved when teachers cannot agree on the scoring or when what teachers do is non-standard, like asking questions which differ in content, form or purpose.

Conversation with a child about the story after taking Running Records adds to the teacher's understanding of the reader in useful ways, and leads the child into discourse about stories.

A record before scoring

The page from Paul's reading (below) could have been made on a blank piece of paper. It shows 55 running words, and was only the first part of the Running Record that was taken. The scoring of errors (E) and self-corrections (SC) on the right-hand side is discussed on pages 65–67. Reread the text to yourself as you think the child read it.

Paul's record

Page of text	Running Record	E	SC
The milk ran	✓ ✓ ✓		
all over the ground.	✓ ✓ ✓ g – | garden ∕ ground |		
And there was the woman	✓ threw | th – | th – | ✓ ✓ R ✓ R₂ there | | T		
with the magpie's tail in her hand.	✓ ✓ ✓ ✓ ✓ ✓		
"Woman, give me back my tail!"	W – | R₄ ✓ g – | get | go ✓ ✓ ✓ ✓ Woman | | give |		
cried the magpie.	✓ ✓ ✓		
"I'll pin it on and fly back	✓ put | pull ✓ ✓ R the | R | SC ✓ ✓ pin | | and | |		
to my mother and father.	✓ ✓ ✓ ✓ ✓		
If you don't give me back my tail	✓ ✓ ✓ ✓ ✓ ✓ ✓		
I'll eat the cabbages in your garden.	✓ ✓ ✓ c – | cabbage | R ✓ ✓ ✓ cabbages | |		

The teacher made this summary:

Generally used meaning at challenging words and often used structure. When approximating he usually checked further, often by rereading, and this sometimes led to self-corrections. Approximations show that he is mainly using initial letters and not searching further. He read with phrasing and retold the story confidently. (Observing him writing might be helpful.)

Scoring of errors and self-corrections

Review the Running Records of the child's behaviour on the book(s) you have selected and consider what was happening as the child read. Consider each error only up to and including the error (not the unread text).

Conventions for scoring

In counting the numbers of errors, some judgements must be made but the following have been found workable.

1   Credit the child with any correct or corrected words.

Child:	to	the	shops	
Text:	for	the	bread	
Score:	✗	✓	✗	[Two errors]

2   There is no penalty for trials which are eventually correct.

A	Child:	want	won't	SC	
	Text:	went			$\begin{bmatrix} \text{No error} \\ \text{One SC} \end{bmatrix}$
	Score:	—	—	✓	

B	Child:	where	we	when	SC	
	Text:	were				$\begin{bmatrix} \text{No error} \\ \text{One SC} \end{bmatrix}$
	Score:	—	—	—	✓	

C	Child:	f –	fet	✓	
	Text:	fright			
	Score:	—	—	✓	[No error]

In example **C** the reader made two attempts to solve the word 'fright', the teacher wrote 'fet' as the best way she could record what she thought he said and then the child reached a solution. This is considered to be solving behaviour and there was no substitution of a word.

3   Insertions add errors so that a child can have more errors than there are words in a line.

Child:	*The*	*train*	*went*	*toot,*	*toot,*	*toot*	
Text:	The	little	engine	sighed	—	—	
Score:	✓	✗	✗	✗	✗	✗	[Five errors]

4   However, the child cannot receive a minus score for a page. The lowest page score is 0.

5   Omissions. If a word, line or sentence is omitted each word is counted as an error. If pages are omitted (perhaps because two pages were turned together) they are not counted as errors. Note that in this case, the number of words on the omitted pages must be deducted from the Running Words Total before calculation.

6   Repeated errors. If the child makes an error (for example 'run' for 'ran') and then substitutes this word repeatedly, it counts as an error every time; but substitution of a proper noun[*] (for example 'Mary' for 'Molly' or 'taxis' for 'Texas') is counted only the first time (even though various alternate substitutions are made).

7   Multiple errors and self-correction. If a child makes two or more errors (for example reads a phrase wrongly) each word is an error. If he then corrects all these errors each corrected word is a self-correction.

8   a) Broken words. Where a word is pronounced as two words (for example a/way) even when this is backed up by pointing as if it were two words, this is regarded as an error of pronunciation not as a reading error, unless what is said is matched to a different word.

b) Childish pronunciations such as 'pitcher' for 'picture' and 'gonna' for 'going to' are counted as correct.

---

[*] Definition of a proper noun: 'In grammar — Applied to a name or noun (written with an initial capital letter) which is used to designate a particular individual object.' (*Oxford Universal Dictionary*, 1973)

9   Inventions defeat the system. When the young child is creatively producing his own version of the story the scoring system finally breaks down and the judgement 'inventing' is recorded for that page, story or book.

10   'Try that again.' When the child is in a tangle this instruction, which does not involve teaching, can be given. It counts as one error and only the second attempt is scored (see page 61).

11   Fewest errors. If there are alternative ways of scoring responses a general principle is to choose the method that gives the fewest possible errors as in B below.

A	Child:	We	went	for	the	bread				
	Text:	You	went	to	the	shop	for	the	bread	
	Score:	✗	✓	✗	✓	✗	✗	✗	✗	[Six errors]

B	Child:	We	went				for	the	bread	
	Text:	You	went	to	the	shop	for	the	bread	
	Score:	✗	✓	✗	✗	✗	✓	✓	✓	[Four errors]

C   Sometimes contractions need to be dealt with under the fewest errors rule. When the reader says 'I'm' for 'I am' or 'dog is' for 'dog's' the fewest errors rule would score the word correct and the contraction part would count as one error.

How to quantify the Running Record

The four boxes on the left provide the calculations corresponding to the steps outlined below. The conversion table provides quick access to accuracy rates.

Step 1: Count the words in the text, omitting titles.

Step 2: Count the errors, and enter the Error Ratio.

Step 3: Use the conversion table to find the Accuracy Rate.

Step 4: Work out the Self-correction Ratio.

Here is one way to think about self-corrections. There were 15 errors in 150 running words of text and the five self-corrections represent an extra five potential errors. Altogether the child made five self-corrections in 20 chances to self-correct.

Step 1

Count the Running Words
150

Step 2

Ratio of Errors to Running Words
$\dfrac{\text{Errors}}{\text{Running Words}}$
$\dfrac{15}{150}$
1 : 10
One in ten

Step 3

Accuracy Rate
$100 - \dfrac{E}{RW} \times \dfrac{100}{1}$
$100 - \dfrac{15}{150} \times \dfrac{100}{1}$
$= 90\%$

Step 4

Self-correction Ratio
$\dfrac{SC}{E + SC}$
$\dfrac{5}{15 + 5}$
1 : 4
One in four

Conversion Table

Error Ratio	Percent Accuracy	
1:200	99.5	
1:100	99	
1:50	98	
1:35	97	
1:25	96	Good opportunities for teachers to observe children's processing of texts
1:20	95	
1:17	94	
1:14	93	
1:12.5	92	
1:11.75	91	
1:10	90	
1:9	89	
1:8	87.5	
1:7	85.5	
1:6	83	The reader tends to lose the support of the meaning of the text
1:5	80	
1:4	75	
1:3	66	
1:2	50	

Turn back to page 64 and score that Running Record. Put one count in the error column for every error and one count in the self-correction column for every self-correction. Total each column and work out the Error Ratio, the Accuracy Rate, and the Self-correction Ratio.

Records for two competent readers

The next two examples capture the reading behaviours of two competent readers and provide the teacher with opportunities to 'read' back from the record what Emma and Claire did. The records are used to introduce an analysis of how the text was read (Interpreting the Running Record, page 71).

Emma read well and there were no self-corrections to analyse on this page of her Running Record. Yet her two errors allowed her teacher to identify two things to talk about. The teacher could talk about the omission of 'as', how what she said sounded right but differed from what the author wrote. Important? Perhaps not. The second discussion could be about how she could work more effectively on the information in the middle of unfamiliar words, which may well be a crucial change in processing which she needs to make.

Emma's record

Analysis of Errors and Self-corrections

Page of Text	Running Record	Information used E M S V	SC M S V
… resting their elbows on it, and talking over its	✓ ✓ ✓ ✓ ✓ ✓ ✓ ✓		
head. "Very uncomfortable for the Dormouse,"	✓. ✓ ✓ ✓ ✓ ✓		
thought Alice; "only as it's asleep, I suppose it	✓ ✓ ✓ —⁄as ✓ ✓ ✓ ✓		
doesn't mind."	✓ ✓.		
The table was a large one, but the three were all	✓ ✓ ✓ ✓ ✓ ✓ ✓ ✓ ✓		
crowded together at one corner of it. "No room!	✓ ✓ ✓ ✓ ✓ ✓. ✓ ✓		
No room!" they cried out when they saw Alice	✓ ✓ ✓ ✓ ✓ ✓ ✓ ✓		
coming. "There's plenty of room!" said Alice	✓. ✓ ✓ ✓ ✓ ✓		
indignantly, and she sat down in a large arm-chair	indently⁄indignantly ✓ ✓ ✓ ✓ ✓ ✓ ✓	M Ⓢ Ⓥ	
at one end of the table.	✓ ✓ ✓ ✓ ✓.		

Although 'indently' is an invented word the 'in———ly' clearly fits a common way of creating an adverb in English; it is a structural feature of the language.

Claire made a number of errors on this text but she often self-corrected without any assistance. (Only a part of the record is shown and I simplified it.)

Claire's record

Analysis of Errors and Self-corrections

Page of Text	Running Record	Information used E (M S V)	SC (M S V)
"Because I'm years older," Hannah smirked.	✓✓✓✓ R ✓✓.		
He gave up arguing and stomped off towards his	✓✓✓✓✓✓✓✓		
room. "See you in the morning," he said to	bedroom / She | SC ✓✓✓✓✓✓ room. / See |	Ⓜ Ⓢ Ⓥ Ⓜ Ⓢ Ⓥ	M S Ⓥ
his mother to emphasize that he was ignoring	✓✓ and | SC emphases ✓ R ✓✓✓ to | emphasize	Ⓜ Ⓢ V M S Ⓥ	M S Ⓥ
Hannah.	Anna | SC Hannah | .	Ⓜ Ⓢ Ⓥ	M S Ⓥ
He posed in front of his bedroom mirror. If	✓ possed ✓✓✓✓✓. ✓ posed	M Ⓢ Ⓥ	
Hannah was a damsel in distress, she couldn't	✓✓✓✓✓ district | SC ✓✓ distress |	M S Ⓥ	M Ⓢ Ⓥ
expect him to come galloping to her rescue.	✓✓✓✓✓✓✓.		
She could stay tied to the stake. He would	✓✓✓ died | SC ✓✓✓. ✓✓ tied |	M S Ⓥ	M Ⓢ Ⓥ
charge in cutting this way and that with his	✓✓✓ the ✓✓✓✓✓ this	M Ⓢ Ⓥ	
fearsome sword. All would fall before him and	✓ s...word| ✓ ✓✓✓✓ sword |		
he would fight his way to where she was tied	✓✓✓✓✓✓✓✓✓		
and then ...	✓✓ ...		

Her teacher summarised the analysis of the reading like this:

Claire is constructing meaningful sentences and is using structure and visual information. She self-corrects most of her errors by picking up more visual information, and attempts all words. In her substitutions she is often using only visual information.

Interpreting the Running Record

There is another level of analysis that will help teachers to work out what information in the text the reader is attending to. To do this you must give closer attention to analysing the error and self-correction behaviours. The analysis takes a little time but it can uncover some important things about the reading process.

Readers of text appear to make decisions about the quality of the message they are getting. One kind of theory would say the child is recalling words and attacking words; another kind of theory would say that the child is using information of various kinds to make a choice among possible responses. He is trying to get the best fit with the limited knowledge he has. ***It is this last kind of theory that guides the following discussion.***

Think about the errors in the record

It is important to analyse every error (looking only at the sentence up to the error) and not look at errors selectively. Ask yourself, 'What led the child to do (or say) that?' For every error ask yourself at least three questions:

> M   Did the meaning or the messages of the text influence the error? Perhaps the reader brought a different meaning to the author's text.

> S   Did the structure (syntax) of the sentence up to the error influence the response? If the error occurs on the first word of the sentence it is marked as positive for structure if the new sentence could have started that way.

> V   Did visual information from the print influence ***any part*** of the error: letter, cluster or word?

(See page 74 for more explanation of the 'V for visual information' category.)

When an error is made write the letters MSV in the error column. Circle the letters if the child's error showed that the child could have been led by meaning or structure or visual information (which will include letter form and/or letter-sound relationships) from the sentence so far.

Scan the record to answer two other questions

1   Did the child's oral language produce the error, with little influence from the print?

2   Was the child clearly getting some phonemic information from the printed letters? What makes you suspect this?

These two questions cannot be used in scoring a record because teachers cannot agree upon their interpretations, and the information is therefore unreliable. However, if the reader sometimes responds as if he was 'just talking', or if specific phonemic information is used, without question, teachers can note these things in their records but do not need to include them in the formal summation of text reading.

Now look at the self-corrections

Often readers make errors and without any prompting, work on the text in some way and self-correct the errors. It is as if they had a feeling that something was not quite right. It is now easy to circle the letters in the self-correction column to record whether the extra information the reader added to make the self-correction was meaning or structure or visual information. This is usually rather interesting, especially when we look at what happens across the entire record. A single error could have been unusual or accidental for the reader.

Consider the pattern of responses

Now look at the overall pattern of the responses you have circled so that you can bring your analysis of errors and self-corrections together into a written summary. This statement about the sources of information used and neglected, and **whether they were used together**, will be useful to guide subsequent teaching.

Record the statement at the top of the Running Record next to the appropriate level of the text. See the completed Running Record sheet on page 73. Note the following:

1   Analysis of the use of meaning and structure and visual information is of little value unless it is done carefully.

2   Consider the sentence only up to the error (not the unread text).

3   Do not try to analyse omissions and insertions.

4   The pattern of M or S or V circled is merely a guide to what is being neglected, what is made a priority, and when the reader can combine different kinds of processing.

5   Avoid analyses for which you have no theoretical support.

RUNNING RECORD SHEET

Name: **Sam** Date: **4.2.11** D. of B.: **1.5.05** Age: **5** yrs **9** mths

School: **Westleigh** Recorder **C.B.**

Text Titles	Errors / Running Words	Error Ratio	Accuracy Rate	Self-correction Ratio
Easy		1:	___ %	1:
Instructional **Dogs (Highgate/P.M.) (seen)**	$\frac{3}{34}$	1: **11.3**	**91** %	1: **2**
Hard		1:	___ %	1:

Directional movement ___ ✓

Analysis of Errors and Self-corrections

Information used or neglected [Meaning (M), Structure or Syntax (S), Visual (V)]

Easy _____

Instructional **Meaning and structure are used predominantly for substitutions with some attention to visual information. Repetition and more visual information led to three self-corrections**

Hard _____

Cross-checking on information (Note that this behaviour changes over time)

Meaning and structure cross-checked with visual information $\frac{dogs}{like}$ $\frac{little}{small}$ Count

Analysis of Errors and Self-corrections

Page	Title: Dogs	E	SC	Information used E MSV	Information used SC MSV
2	$\frac{s-}{Some\|T}$ ✓ ✓ ✓	I		M S Ⓥ	
3	✓ ✓ ✓ ✓				
4	✓ ✓ ✓ $\frac{scary}{growly}$	I		Ⓜ Ⓢ V	
5	✓ $\frac{dogs\|R\|SC}{like\|\|}$ ✓ ✓		I	Ⓜ Ⓢ V	M S Ⓥ
6	✓ ✓ ✓ ✓				
7	✓ ✓ ✓ $\frac{little\|R\|SC}{small\|\|}$		I	Ⓜ Ⓢ V	M S Ⓥ
8	✓ ✓ $\frac{dog\ is\|R\|SC}{dog's\|\|}$ ✓ ✓		I	Ⓜ Ⓢ Ⓥ	M S Ⓥ
	✓ ✓ $\frac{biggest\|R\|A\|}{cuddliest\|\|\|T}$ ✓ ✓	I		Ⓜ Ⓢ V	
		3	3		

Read slowly with some intonation.

Understanding the reading process

When teachers ask themselves 'What does my record tell me?' they bring their own beliefs about literacy (their personal theory of literacy learning) and their background of professional experience into the interpretation. Interpretations of Running Records are heavily weighted with the theoretical view the teacher already holds. My interpretations fit with my theory that progress depends on an increasing complexity in the processing which enables the reader to read more difficult texts. I think of the child as working with several different types of knowledge about print (which I call 'different kinds of information').

To explain the error consider the behaviour that might have led the child up to the point of the error.

To explain a self-correction consider what might have led the child to spontaneously correct the error.

When teachers have different theories about what is important for the beginning reader to learn they could interpret the same behaviour record in different ways. They may ask quite different questions of the data because they emphasise the importance of different things. Extensive research into what young readers do as they read text and careful training of teachers as observers ensure that behaviour records will look the same even though teacher interpretations might differ.

For example, examine the attention given in these analyses to 'V' standing for the visual information in print. During acquisition the visual information becomes intricately linked to phonemic information (the sounds of speech or phonology) so that children could probably be said to 'hear' a letter or cluster of letters they are looking at. Theorists tell us that visual information also links directly to a vocabulary of known words (spelling patterns or orthography). So, theoretically, the symbol V in the analysis of Running Records stands for the stimulus information on the page of print irrespective of whether the processing is through a phonological system or a visual system. This is a point at which teachers might differ in their 'understanding' of what a reader was doing.

What if a reliable behaviour record does not support expectations? Unable to deny that the actual behaviour did occur we probably need to adjust any of our assumptions that are not supported by recorded data. So it is important that we have reliable records.

Running Records are useful if we remember the following things.

- Record error behaviour in full because the information is needed when interpreting the records.

- Poor observation will reduce the number of errors and inflate the accuracy score.

- Reliability drops as accuracy levels fall because there is more error to be recorded.

- Observation of poor readers is difficult and rigorous training is required to reach agreement on scoring because of the complexity of the error behaviour.

- The most reliable records would be obtained by scoring an observation immediately following its manual recording but for classroom teachers that is not usually possible.

In older readers look for different signs of progress

If Running Records are used with older readers *there should be a special reason for taking them.* They are excellent for recording the early phases of literacy acquisition but before long what the reader is doing becomes too fast and too sophisticated for teachers to observe in real time. Literacy processing shifts gradually towards this.

Some of the changes to look for in older readers are these.

- It is an important 'sign of progress' when errors contain several kinds of correct information even though the final decision is not quite correct. As the reader learns to process more information more quickly, behaviours change and new things can be noted. Errors occur even though the reader clearly used meaning and structure and visual information to get to a response (for example, 'strong' for 'sturdy').

- Another change occurs when more proficient readers utter only the word beginning and then give the whole word. These are examples:

  wu/would   pl/play   Pe/Peter   bu/but

- A similar kind of thing happens when the older reader corrects what might have been an error before giving the whole word, as in:

  m…/parents   gar…/ground   d…/tied

- Sometimes there is more repetition as the older reader tries to regroup words in phrases.

- In older readers self-correction occurs less frequently. In theory we suppose that it has 'gone underground' and the reader is correcting errors before saying them. If the teacher introduces a more challenging text the process of self-correcting may reappear. Even adults reading aloud can be heard to self-correct.

Records of individual and group progress

Education is primarily concerned with change in the learning of individuals, yet educators rarely document change over time in individuals as they learn. It is not difficult to collect evidence of change over time in early literacy learning, particularly from young children at the beginning of formal education.

Three ways of using Running Records to capture individual progress over time are shown.

- In Rochelle's case the teacher grouped the books that her class read into approximate levels of difficulty and placed numbers for these levels at the left side of her sheet. Then she took Running Records of Rochelle's reading on two occasions several months apart, and entered the names of the books Rochelle found easy, instructional or hard. Rochelle's progress is clear.

- A different record was kept by the teacher who was keeping a close watch on Joan's progress by monitoring it frequently. This teacher used the Record of Book Level sheet (page 79) and entered the date of the observation along the horizontal line. She chose to take a record once a week. She entered an open circle for the instructional level of text read, because no story at a higher level of text reached the 90 percent accuracy criterion. The next week she raised the text difficulty level and Joan's accuracy fell below 90 percent and so she used a black circle on her graph. In two more weeks of teaching she raised the difficulty level again. (Meanwhile Joan read several new texts but all at the same level of difficulty.) From then onwards as the teacher raised the text difficulty Joan was able to take the challenge except for once after a holiday break.

- A teacher can follow several different children, using the same plotting procedures. There are problems of clustering if the children are homogeneous in their progress. Graphs of progress made for a group of children will show individual differences in starting levels, in paths of progress, in fast or slow 'take-off' in the programme and in final outcome levels. The teacher would quickly identify children who were working on material that was too difficult, preventing them from working in the context of mostly correct reading, or children who temporarily needed more of her attention. This is one way to monitor the progress of a group.

Rochelle's progress at two observation points

Book Level	Progress
1	
2	
3	
4	
5	Time 1 (date)
6	*The Escalator* (easy)
7	*Going to School* (instructional)
8	*Playtime* (hard)
9	
10	
11	
12	Time 2 (date)
13	*The Pet Show* (easy)
14	*A Wet Morning* (instructional)
15	*Hungry Lambs* (hard)
16	
17	
18	
19	

A weekly record of Joan's progress

Teachers may follow the progress of several children

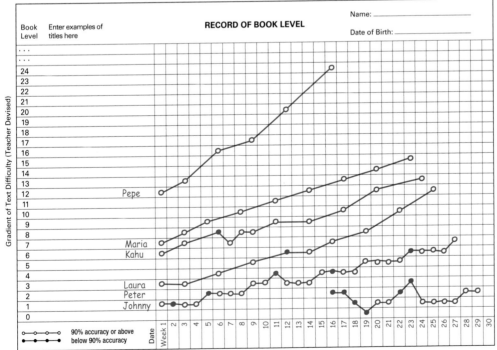

A different way to take a record of progress is shown below. A child's progress through a series of reading book levels was listed from first to last along some gradient of difficulty and the accuracy with which each book was read was recorded. Day by day or week by week a child's increasing control over text reading is captured on this record. It is reassuring to know that progress is being made as time passes. When that kind of record is also backed by an analysis of the literacy processing behaviours of the reader from time to time, teachers in classrooms and early intervention teachers have a tool for monitoring changes in how the reader works on the text, what the reader is noticing, what is easy, what is confusing, and what needs the teacher's attention.

An individual record of books read over 28 weeks

Week	Book title (publisher series) Key: R to R — Ready to Read series PM — Price Milburn series	Level	Accuracy	Rating	Self-correction rate
1	*Nick's Glasses* (R to R)	10	98%	Easy	1:1.3
2	*Breakfast* (Young Shorty)	12	94%	Inst.	1:2.5
3	*Mark Fox* (Young Shorty)	14	96%	Easy	1:2
4	*The Hat Trick* (Bangers & Mash)	13	98%	Easy	1:1
5	*Burglars* (Young Shorty)	15	93%	Inst.	1:2
6	*Burglars* (Young Shorty)	15	96%	Easy	1:1.3
7	*Wet Days at School* (City Kids)	14	98%	Easy	1:2
8	*Buster is Lost* (Lang. in Action)	15	94%	Inst.	1:2
9	*My Ghost* (Mount Gravatt)	15	95%	Easy	1:2
10	*A Hat for Pedro* (Pedro Books)	14	95%	Easy	1:1.5
11	*Pedro and the Cars* (Pedro Books)	15	90%	Inst.	1:3
12	*Monster Looks for a Friend* (Monster Books)	16	98%	Easy	1:1.3
13	*Pot of Gold* (Scott Foresman)	16	96%	Easy	1:1.5
14	*Giant's Hiccups* (Open Highways)	17	96%	Easy	1:2
15	*Monster and the Magic Umbrella* (Monster Books)	18	97%	Easy	1:1.3
16	*Chocolate Shop* (Young Shorty)	18	94%	Inst.	1:2
17	*Beauty and the Bus* (Hart-Davis)	18	94%	Inst.	1:2
18	*Magpie's Tail* (R to R)	19	98%	Easy	1:2
19	*Poached Eggs* (Hart-Davis)	19	94%	Inst.	1:2
20	*Monster at School* (Monster Books)	19	97%	Easy	1:1.5
21	*Won and Lost* (Young Shorty)	20	96%	Easy	1:2
22	*The Hairy Boggart* (Story Box)	22	98%	Easy	1:1.4
23	*Gotham Way of Counting* (R to R)	23	93%	Inst.	1:2.6
24	*The Greedy Cook and the Hungry Shark* (N.F.S. School Journal)	24	97%	Easy	1:1.3
25	*Only a Little Fire* (PM)	25	97%	Easy	Nil
26	(No record taken)				
27	*Having a Haircut* (City Kids)	24	94%	Inst.	1:2
28	*The Old Car* (PM)	25	95%	Easy	1:1.75

RECORD OF BOOK LEVEL

Name: _____

Date of Birth: _____

Gradient of Text Difficulty (Teacher Devised)

Book Level	Enter examples of titles here
⋮	
⋮	
24	
23	
22	
21	
20	
19	
18	
17	
16	
15	
14	
13	
12	
11	
10	
9	
8	
7	
6	
5	
4	
3	
2	
1	
0	

● 90% accuracy or above
○ below 90% accuracy

Date

Weekly Observations

Many uses for Running Records

Some suggestions for using Running Records in classroom settings could be the following.

School entry checks

Teachers will have their own ways of collecting and recording information about learners from the time they enter school. Running Records can even be taken on the child's earliest attempts to read little books, enriching the teacher's observations.

Running Records on simple books would only be useful for assessing children who had a rich preparation for beginning school. For children who had limited opportunities to learn about literacy before beginning school Running Records would be best delayed until schools had provided suitable literacy experiences.

Education systems tend to be highly selective about what they use for a baseline assessment of literacy processes. However, instead of limiting observations to a measure of letter knowledge (which is common) teachers could use a range of tasks because they would be more likely to capture the areas that reveal the strengths of individual children. The Observation Survey is such a broad-ranging assessment.

For teaching individuals

Using the Running Record for teaching purposes teachers might:

- first try to find a book level appropriate for a child, then try an easier book and a harder book

- check a child after a series of lessons

- evaluate whether a lift in text level is appropriate

- observe particular difficulties in particular children in order to modify instructional emphases

- evaluate in order to place a child in an appropriate instructional group, class or school

- add to a record which is monitoring an individual's progress over time.

For teaching groups

Using the Running Record for informing group instruction:

- teachers might group children who could work together

- teachers could evaluate progress and see when regrouping is desirable

- teachers would see how different the processing of particular children was and give attention to an individual learner at the time of the group instruction.

Running Records can be used with older readers, provided oral reading is what we want to observe (Johnston, 1996, 2000).

Evidence of emphasis: what things get attention in your programme?

If teachers take records of text reading with a wide sample of children they will quickly discover which things are emphasised and neglected in their class instruction:

- word-by-word reading

- sounding out words in single phonemes

- not attending to meaning and reading nonsense

- ignoring first-letter cues or not going beyond these

- not attending to detail in the middle of a word.

If any of these persist longer than they should they may show up as a problem for a group of learners. On the other hand good outcomes may show up. Most of the children:

- get it all together smoothly

- work on new words in ways that surprise and impress the teacher

- enjoy the stories and are able to discuss features of those stories

- show improved control over structure in phrased reading.

If the programme is changed so that new emphases are introduced, like a shift to asking for more fluent, phrased reading, or teaching readers how to approach multi-syllabic words with several unstressed vowels, then Running Records can be used to monitor whether any changes that are made to instruction are having the desired effect. Running Records can help teachers improve the reading of individuals, but they can also be used for planning and monitoring shifts in the instruction delivered in classrooms.

RUNNING RECORD SHEET

Name: _____ Date: _____ D. of B.: _____ Age: _____ yrs _____ mths

School: _____ Recorder: _____

Text Titles		Errors / Running Words	Error Ratio	Accuracy Rate	Self-correction Ratio
Easy	_____	_____	1: _____	_____ %	1: _____
Instructional	_____	_____	1: _____	_____ %	1: _____
Hard	_____	_____	1: _____	_____ %	1: _____

Directional movement _____

Analysis of Errors and Self-corrections
Information used or neglected [Meaning (M), Structure or Syntax (S), Visual (V)]

Easy _____

Instructional _____

_____

Hard _____

_____

Cross-checking on information (Note that this behaviour changes over time)

Page	Title	Count		Analysis of Errors and Self-corrections
		E	SC	**Information used**
				E MSV / SC MSV

Page		Count		Analysis of Errors and Self-corrections	
		E	SC	Information used	
				E MSV	SC MSV

6 Observation task for Letter Identification

Letter Identification

An alphabet may contain as few as 30 letters (see Maori below with 33) or more than 60 or 70 symbols. A child beginning literacy education in English will encounter 26 lower case letters, 26 upper case letters, and two common ways of writing 'a' and 'g', making a total score of 54 symbols to test.

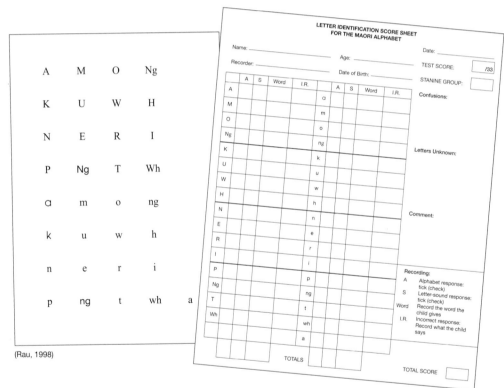

A	M	O	Ng
K	U	W	H
N	E	R	I
P	Ng	T	Wh
a	m	o	ng
k	u	w	h
n	e	r	i
p	ng	t	wh	a

(Rau, 1998)

Letter Identification Task for the Maori alphabet, which contains 33 letters

The following early writing sample (Clay, 1987) illustrates how few letters the school entrant may be able to write and how specific to the individual that knowledge is.

It was common practice for teachers to begin the teaching of letters alphabetically. This seemed to be a neat and efficient way to go. It is more effective however to find out which letters the child knows and then seek a fast route to his learning the others. When teachers understand this faster route to learning they find ways to monitor individual progress to ensure that all letters are learned.

If children have paid little attention to print in their preschool years they will need to learn to distinguish between the symbols of the alphabet after they come to school. Rather slowly they will begin to notice what makes one symbol different from another. A teacher wrote down what one boy dictated — 'My Daddy is a builder'. From his attempt to copy the teacher's model we can observe several problems he is having.

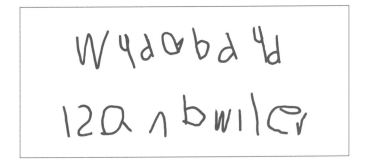

Learning to see how the symbols of any alphabet are different one from another is a huge learning task. Learning to recognise the identity of a symbol's shape is different from two other kinds of learning — learning to write that symbol or learning to link it to a sound or phoneme.

Using the Letter Identification observation task

Administration

Assess all letters, lower case and upper case. Make this a standard task, the same for every child, by using the large print alphabet on page 87. It could be copied from the book and mounted on card for this purpose. Ensure that the child reads across the lines so that the letters are treated in a random order (*and not in alphabetical order*). This observation task should take from 5 to 10 minutes. Use the questions on page 86 (and only these questions) to get the child to respond to the letters. Do not ask only for sounds, or names or for words that begin with the letter or sound.

The task is designed to find out which alphabetic symbols the children are noticing. *A name, or a sound, or a word beginning with the letter or sound, are all acceptable signs that the child is identifying a letter in some way*, and that is the first hurdle.

Only one of the three ways of distinguishing letters needs to be given by the child. Attaching a second or third label to the letter will be easy once the letter has been distinguished from all other letters. (In the Maori language in most cases the sound of the letter is also the name of the letter.)

To introduce the task say to the child:
- *What do you call these?*
- *Can you find some that you know?*

Point to each letter in horizontal lines. Say:
- *What is this one?*

If a child does not respond use one or more of these questions:
Try to avoid bias towards any one of them.
- *Do you know its name?*
- *What sound does it make?*
- *Do you know a word that starts like that?*

Then moving to other letters. Say:
- *What is this? And this?*

If the child hesitates start with the first letter of his name, and then go to the first line. Point to every letter in turn to keep the child's attention on the task and work across the lines. Use a masking card if necessary.

Recording and scoring

- Use the Letter Identification Score Sheet (see page 88) and mark the A column for an alphabetical response, the S column for sound, or the Word column for a word beginning with that letter. Use a tick or check (✓) for the correct response. When the response is incorrect, record what the child says in the I.R. column (for Incorrect Response).

- Score as correct:
  — either an alphabet name
  — or a sound that is acceptable for that letter
  — or a response which says 'it begins like', giving a word for which that letter is the initial letter or sound.

- Find the subtotals for each kind of response — alphabetical, sound and word beginning.

- Total the child's score adding all three types of response together and consult the stanine tables.

A	F	K	P	W	Z
B	H	O	J	U	
C	Y	L	Q	M	
D	N	S	X	I	
E	G	R	V	T	
a	f	k	p	w	z
b	h	o	j	u	a
c	y	l	q	m	
d	n	s	x	i	
e	g	r	v	t	g

LETTER IDENTIFICATION SCORE SHEET
(ENGLISH)

Date: _____

Name: _____   Age: _____   TEST SCORE: [/54]

Recorder: _____   Date of Birth: _____   STANINE GROUP: [   ]

	A	S	Word	I.R.		A	S	Word	I.R.
A					ɑ				
F					f				
K					k				
P					p				
W					w				
Z					z				
B					b				
H					h				
O					o				
J					j				
U					u				
					a				
C					c				
Y					y				
L					l				
Q					q				
M					m				
D					d				
N					n				
S					s				
X					x				
I					i				
E					e				
G					g				
R					r				
V					v				
T					t				
					g				
			TOTALS						

Confusions:

Letters Unknown:

Comment:

Recording:

A   Alphabet response: tick (check)

S   Letter-sound response: tick (check)

Word   Record the word the child gives

I.R.   Incorrect response: Record what the child says

TOTAL SCORE [   ]

Stanine scores

To compare the child's performance with that of other children use one of the tables of scores below. In this book each task has four age tables. Select the table which will allow you to compare the child's score with those of other children of his age (see page 126). Look up the total raw score obtained by the child you assessed on the age table that is right for him and read from the second line of boxes his scaled score, a number between 1 and 9. This scaled score is called a stanine and it provides a guide to how well the child compares with a sample of 796 New Zealand children in February 2000. If the score on the table is allocated across more than one stanine group choose the lowest value: that is, be conservative rather than generous.

Immediately preceding the summary of the Observation Survey results (Chapter 10, pages 126–128), readers will find a general discussion of stanine scores, why they are used, when they are helpful and what their limitations are. (See pages 155–160 for stanine scores for Canada, the United Kingdom and the United States.)

LETTER IDENTIFICATION STANINES FOR FOUR AGE GROUPS

Letter Identification: 5.00 – 5.50 years
(N = 223; Score Range: 0–54; Mean = 39.0; SE = 1.05; SD = 15.7)

Test Score	0–3	4–12	13–27	28–42	43–49	50–52	53	– 54 –	
Stanine Grp	1	2	3	4	5	6	7	8	9

Letter Identification: 5.51 – 6.00 years
(N = 170; Score Range: 0–54; Mean = 46.6; SE = 0.93; SD = 12.1)

Test Score	0–10	11–35	36–46	47–51	52	53	––– 54 –––		
Stanine Grp	1	2	3	4	5	6	7	8	9

Letter Identification: 6.01 – 6.50 years
(N = 230; Score Range: 0–54; Mean = 50.7; SE = 0.50; SD = 7.5)

Test Score	0–34	35–48	49–50	51	52	53	––– 54 –––		
Stanine Grp	1	2	3	4	5	6	7	8	9

Letter Identification: 6.51 – 7.00 years
(N = 173; Score Range: 0–54; Mean = 51.6; SE = 0.49; SD = 6.4)

Test Score	0–40	41–50	51–52	53		–––– 54 ––––			
Stanine Grp	1	2	3	4	5	6	7	8	9

(For more technical information see Appendices.)

Interpreting Letter Identification scores

The record form contains information which can be used to guide instruction. It shows:

- the child's preferred mode of identifying letters

- the letters a child confuses (so that they can be kept apart in the teaching programme)

- the unknown letters

- and comments about the child's responding.

Following the observations, teaching should aim to improve the child's ability to distinguish letters one from another:

- at first on any basis that works, including but not limited to letter-sound relationships, and work to expand the child's range of known letters

- as more and more letters are controlled children become ready for systematic associations like alphabetical names or sound equivalents. When they know most of the letters they are more able to be flexible and can consider alternative ways of labelling letters.

As it is possible and necessary for young children to completely master the particular set of letters in a language, one would expect a child to move gradually over time through the stanine score range until he reached perfect scoring for the symbols of the alphabet. An individual child's stanine score indicates his status relative to all children in the age group. Of particular value is the comparison of a child's scores at two points of time because this captures how much progress that child has made in the intervening period.

High progress children not only master the identification of all letters but after a year or so at school they can easily produce 54 letter names, 54 letter sounds and 54 words beginning with the letter. They have a broad foundation in letter learning which they can deal with in flexible ways.

However, Letter Identification scores are sensitive to instructional procedures. Focused teaching of letter-sound relationships will result in responses to the items being mostly sounds rather than names, and the whole set of letters may be learned earlier or later under different kinds of instruction. This is another reason why it is preferable to accept *any* of the three ways of distinguishing letters at first, because the teaching programme may have turned the children's scoring towards one kind of responding; and any way of identifying the symbols is valuable in the beginning. On pages 91–92 there is a discussion of another way to use this alphabet to assess letter-sound relationships.

Limited prediction from Letter Identification

From time to time I have been asked for an opinion about using the Letter Identification task in a research project but assessing only some of the letters. It is seen as one of the better predictors of literacy progress for school entrants in longitudinal research. I offer the following comments on this practice.

- Letter Identification is not a stand-alone indicator of preparation for literacy learning.

- Letter names are a limited way of testing what children know about letters.

- Picking and choosing letters and not assessing the whole set may miss half of what some children know.

- This observation task is designed not for predicting progress but to find out what children do and do not know, to be used as a guide for subsequent teaching.

- If the plan were to compare alphabet knowledge across two languages or scripts, careful thought should be given to whether differences exist in the number and range of symbols in the two languages, and to the frequency of symbol use in each language.

Cautions about assessing letter-sound relationships

If you are a teacher who feels unable to teach children unless they know all the letter-sound relationships first, you may want to repeat the Letter Identification assessment on another day and this time say to the child, 'What sound does this letter make?' *This makes the task harder, and being able to do this comes later than the standard procedure recommended above, asking, 'What is this one?'* It is one way of knowing letters. It is not a measurement of all the knowledge that the child can bring to his early lessons. While not a formal requirement of the survey, testing for 'sounds' can be done later if the teacher needs to know about this.

In answer to the question 'What sound does this letter make?', one large-scale study in New Zealand of Reading Recovery children distinguished two sets of sounds for letters:

1) a large easy-to-learn group

B b C D d F f G g g H h J j K k L M m N n O o P p R r S s T t V v W w Z z

2) a smaller hard-to-learn group

A ɑ a c   E e   i l I l   Q q   U u   X x   Y y

The hard-to-learn group of sounds for letters are easily confused for a variety of reasons but often because to children beginning their formal literacy learning they seem to have similar visual features which must be distinguished. Children who are learning to write at the same time as they are learning to read find the motor movement of writing helps to distinguish the letters which seemed at first to be similar.

The most difficult sounds for letters (percent of children making an error) were rather surprising.

U (37%)   q (36%)   u (35%)   x (34%)   X (33%)   Y (19%)   Q (18%)   y (17%)

This kind of evidence points to the importance of the visual features in contributing significantly to establishing letter-sound associations. It suggests that curricula that begin with A and work through to Z as a teaching order are ignoring easier ways to sequence learning.

It is surprising to look at the *error* percentages of sounds for letters for what is commonly thought of as the most confusing set of letters.

P	B	D	Q		p	b	d	q
0%	1%	1%	18%		1%	3%	6%	36%

Most of the poor readers who were selected for an early intervention knew many letter-sound relationships at the beginning of their supplementary programme, and by the end there were only a few tricky ones left to learn.

An early awareness of alphabetic knowledge

This example of exploring the alphabet came from a child not yet four years of age. Sally-Ann made a list of 'all the letters I know'. In the sixth row after '+ + B' she begins the alphabet at E and, give or take a few hitches, gets to W. This was the first time her parents had seen Q, ɑ, K, V, or W in her work (Clay, 1987).

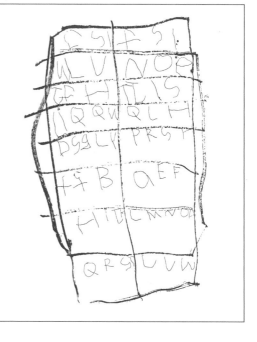

7 Observation task for Word Reading

Word Reading

Standardised word tests used to measure reading achievement are based on the principle of sampling from the child's reading vocabulary. This cannot be a reliable approach until a child has acquired sufficient vocabulary to make sampling a feasible measurement strategy.

For early identification a different approach is required. The principle then is to sample words from that restricted corpus of words which the child has had some opportunities to learn. Any assessment of first-year instruction must be closely linked to that instruction. Word lists are compiled from the high frequency words in the reading materials that have been used in the school. The most frequently occurring words in the series of reading texts being used will probably provide a satisfactory source of test items. (See below for discussion of how such a test might be constructed from reading vocabulary to which the young learners have already been exposed.)

The Word Reading task was devised for children who were using the New Zealand Ready to Read series (first published in 1963 and revised regularly since 1978). A list of 15 words systematically sampled from the 45 most frequently occurring words in the 12 little books of the Ready to Read series, proved to be a very good instrument for ranking or grouping children during the first year of instruction and for low progress readers in the second year (Clay, 1966). Three alternative word lists are available. New norms for these three lists were obtained for New Zealand children in 2000.

Using the Word Reading observation task

Administration

The Word Reading task takes about two minutes to administer. The task sheet on page 95 may be copied and mounted on card.

Ask the child to read one list. Use List A or List B or List C. The other lists may be covered with a card. (Use alternative lists for re-assessment. Do not use the lists for teaching.)

To introduce the task, point to the practice word and say to the child:

- *What is this word?*

Tell the child the practice word if necessary and never score it. Do not help with any other words.

Then, point to each word in turn. Say:

- *What is this word?*
- *And this one?*

If the child does not respond to a word, move to the next one. Say:

- *What is this word?*

Recording and scoring

Use the Word Reading Score Sheet on page 96 and mark each correct response with a tick (check). Record any incorrect response beside the word. If the child corrects a word record the incorrect response and write SC (self-correction) beside it. Score the word as correct.

Total the child's score of correct responses and consult the stanine table.

The score will indicate the extent to which a child is accumulating a reading vocabulary of the most frequently used words in the Ready to Read series during his first year at school. Scores should move gradually from low to high levels over that first year. The scores may be used, together with teachers' observations recorded for book reading, for grouping children. Successive tests will indicate whether a progressive change is occurring in the child's reading of words.

(The procedures above are applicable to the Word Reading tasks on page 98.)

Stanine scores

To compare the child's performance with that of other children use one of the tables of scores on page 97. In this book each task has four age tables. Select the table which will allow you to compare the child's score with those of other children of his age (see page 126). Look up the total raw score obtained by the child you assessed on the age table that is right for him and read from the second line of boxes his scaled score, a number between 1 and 9. This scaled score is called a stanine and it provides a guide to how well the child compares with a sample of 796 New Zealand children in February 2000. If the score on the table is allocated across more than one stanine group choose the lowest value: that is, be conservative rather than generous.

LIST A Practice Word the	LIST B Practice Word said	LIST C Practice Word is
I	and	Father
Mother	to	come
are	will	for
here	look	a
me	he	you
shouted	up	at
am	like	school
with	in	went
car	where	get
children	Mr	we
help	going	they
not	big	ready
too	go	this
meet	let	boys
away	on	please

WORD READING SCORE SHEET

Use any **one** list of words

Date: _____

Name: _____

Age: _____ Date of Birth: _____

Recorder: _____

TEST SCORE: [ ] /15

STANINE GROUP: [ ]

Record incorrect responses beside word

LIST **A**	LIST **B**	LIST **C**
I	and	Father
Mother	to	come
are	will	for
here	look	a
me	he	you
shouted	up	at
am	like	school
with	in	went
car	where	get
children	Mr	we
help	going	they
not	big	ready
too	go	this
meet	let	boys
away	on	please

CLAY WORD READING STANINES FOR FOUR AGE GROUPS

Clay Word Reading: 5.00 – 5.50 years
(N = 223; Score Range: 0–15; Mean = 4.3; SE = 0.30; SD = 4.5)

Test Score	— 0 —		1	2	3–4	5–8	9–11	12–14	15
Stanine Grp	1	2	3	4	5	6	7	8	9

Clay Word Reading: 5.51 – 6.00 years
(N = 170; Score Range: 0–15; Mean = 7.7; SE = 0.39; SD = 5.11)

Test Score	0	1	2–3	4–6	7–10	11–13	14	— 15 —	
Stanine Grp	1	2	3	4	5	6	7	8	9

Clay Word Reading: 6.01 – 6.50 years
(N = 230; Score Range: 0–15; Mean = 11.4; SE = 0.28; SD = 4.3)

Test Score	0–1	2–4	5–9	10–12	13–14	———— 15 ————			
Stanine Grp	1	2	3	4	5	6	7	8	9

Clay Word Reading: 6.51 – 7.00 years
(N = 173; Score Range: 0–15; Mean = 13.0; SE = 0.24; SD = 3.1)

Test Score	0–4	5–10	11–12	13	14	———— 15 ————			
Stanine Grp	1	2	3	4	5	6	7	8	9

(For more technical information see Appendices.)

Immediately preceding the summary of the Observation Survey results (Chapter 10, pages 126–128), readers will find a general discussion of stanine scores, why they are used, when they are helpful and what their limitations are. (See pages 155–160 for stanine scores for Canada, the United Kingdom and the United States.)

One would expect children to completely master this learning and move through the stanine score range until they reach near-perfect scoring. Slips and measurement errors may be responsible for less than perfect scores. Every score you calculate will be surrounded by a band of potential measurement error.

Interpreting Word Reading scores

What the Word Reading task does not do:

- It does not give a reading age.

- It does not discriminate so well between better readers after one year of instruction. On the contrary it groups them together.

- Differences of less than three score points are not sufficiently reliable to support any decisions about the child's progress, without other evidence.

- It does not sample a child's Word Reading if he is working beyond the level of early reading books.

Other 'first' word reading tests (Canberra, Ohio, Duncan)

To support the use of this Observation Survey in Australia and in the United States two other assessments of word reading have been constructed. These two tests were designed in different ways. The Canberra Word Test was developed for use with Australian children by Clough, McIntyre and Cowey (1990), following closely the model used to construct the 'Ready to Read' Word Reading task but using as a source the high frequency words in reading materials used in Canberra schools in 1989. The reading books published under the series titles 'Sunshine' and 'Storybox' form the bulk of the reading material from which the words were drawn. Teachers may find that the Canberra Word Test is suitable for use in other countries where 'Sunshine' and 'Storybox' books are used.

The Ohio Word Test is republished in Appendix 7 to this book (pages 195–196) with the permission of the authors. It was constructed in a different way, using the high frequency words from the Dolch Word List; the method of construction is described in Pinnell, Lyons, Young and Deford (1987). The administration procedures are the same as those used in the 'Ready to Read' Word Reading task.

The Duncan Word Test, developed in a research project, is described in Duncan and McNaughton (2001). It used words from more recently published first reading books placed in two lists of 23 words. This was included in the assessment battery from which the new Observation Survey stanine scores were calculated for a representative sample of schools and a random sample of children in 2000. The normative assessment administered in 2000 showed the Clay and Duncan tests to be equally valuable on all the test statistics. There was no difference between the measurement qualities of the Clay and Duncan lists; they could be considered optional alternates, and correlations between the two measures for four age groups were 0.90 and above. The three original 15-word lists have been retained because they are shorter and provide more options for the more frequent assessment needed in early interventions.

Other reading tests (Burt, Neale, STAR)

Once the child who entered school at five years has a reading level of 6:0 to 6:6 then standardised tests typically used by a school system begin to measure the achievement of average and better than average readers reliably. However they remain unhelpful for guiding the instruction of the lowest achievers.

The Burt Word Reading Test (NZCER, 1981) is widely used in New Zealand where it is a standardised assessment of reading before eight or nine years. Like the Canberra Word Test, the Ohio Word Test or the British Abilities Scale Word Test, the Burt Word Reading Test cannot describe the child's integrated system of reading behaviours observed when reading continuous text. However, like any word reading test it will rank children on knowledge of words in isolation and has quite a strong correlation with text reading when predicting group achievement. It is a more questionable indicator of the progress made by individual children and should be considered alongside a measure of text reading.

The local standardisation of the Burt Word Reading Test by the New Zealand Council of Educational Research in 1981 provided a nationally normed word test for New Zealand children. Children's level of attainment is placed within an age band rather than using the concept of a reading age (allowing for the variations that occur in testing which create measurement error).

Historically, in many early New Zealand studies another British word test, the Schonell Word Reading Test, was used because research demonstrated clearly that the score for the Clay Word Test of 15 words (described earlier) could be added to the score for the first 30 words of the Schonell R1 test to give a combined score which was psychometrically a good measure of reading of New Zealand children between five and seven years at that time (Clay, 1966).

In most countries one of the normative word tests commonly used in schools can be given together with the Observation Survey tasks to provide two kinds of information.

- A sample of the reader's competence with reading words in isolation.

- A comparison with the normative performance of the child's age group.

To assess children reading continuous text teachers could use a standardised oral reading test which uses paragraphs or short extracts, like the Neale Analysis of Reading Ability (Neale, 1958; ACER, 1988; NFER-Nelson, 1989). It is useful to supplement the normative assessment as described by Neale with Running Record-type observations of the oral reading of paragraphs. A teacher who has thought about the reading process can extract more information about the child's system of operating on the information in print from a Running Record on a paragraph reading test than is yielded only by the standardised test scores. Records of the child's text-reading behaviour on graded paragraphs in a situation which is standard and which is graded in difficulty can be useful after the first year or two of school instruction.

The STAR Reading Test, 2nd Edition (Elley et al, 2011) is a revision of the former Supplementary Tests of Achievement in Reading. The revision was undertaken by the original author, Warwick Elley, with a team from the New Zealand Council for Educational Research. It is designed to assess student progress and achievement in reading from the beginning of Year 3 to the beginning of Year 9. STAR consists of four sub-tests that assess Word Recognition, Sentence Comprehension, Paragraph Comprehension (using the 'matching cloze' format for students in Years 3 and 4 and the 'cloze procedure' for all other students), and Vocabulary Range. STAR has an additional two sub-tests for Year 7 to 9 students.

8 Observation task for Writing Vocabulary

Writing Vocabulary

An introduction to the writing process is provided in Chapter 2. The Cinderella of the literacy world is surely early writing. There are probably many reasons why it is neglected but the most obvious is a common belief that children must learn to read before they learn to spell and then subsequently they will learn to write.

Studies of preschool children have dispelled this illusion. Before three- and four-year-olds have even begun to wonder how the words of their favourite story can be 'read' to them, they notice print in their environment, scribble and make letters on paper. They explore print before they explore the act of reading. Many interesting studies have reported what it is that children notice (Chomsky, 1972; Bissex, 1980; Goodman, 1990; Dyson, 1997; Kress, 2000).

Most children have a small repertoire of 'writing behaviour' when they enter school. For about six months after entry to school the changes in writing behaviours of New Zealand five-year-olds are not spectacular. However, in the second six months of literacy instruction a sudden increase in pace of learning about writing was captured in an early research study by Robinson (1973), and in normative testing carried out in New Zealand in 2000 the trend is still clear. (See Writing Vocabulary stanine tables page 109.) After about six months at school both boys and girls begin to make rapid gains in the numbers of words (correctly spelled) which they can write. This occurs in an instructional situation where children are invited to write daily and are helped by teachers to put their messages in print, but where learning how to spell words is not a feature. During their introduction to literacy, and in a classroom rich with evidence of how we can use both reading and writing, children are catching on to some of the features of words and messages written down.

By observing children as they write we can learn a great deal about what features of print they are attending to. Writing behaviour is a good indicator of a child's knowledge of letters and of the left-to-right sequencing behaviour required to read English. In writing words letter by letter the child must recall not only the configuration but also the details of letter formation and letter order. A child's written texts are a good source of information about his visual discrimination of print for as the child learns to write words, the hand and the eye will support and supplement each other as the learner discovers how to distinguish different letters one from another (which is a very large set of visual discrimination learning in any language).

Discuss this example of Kelly's writing with a colleague. Does the child make some well-formed letters? How many letter forms can you recognise? Does she have a small stock of words which she can construct from memory? Does she get the letters correctly sequenced? Specifically, what are the letters she knows? What is she confusing?

Reading seems to help writing and writing seems to help reading, especially in the first year of literacy instruction. They work together reciprocally, one boosting the other. How? We may never explain how, in the brain, one activity boosts the effectiveness of another, but we can think how good car drivers monitor the world through the windscreen and take in information from rear vision and side mirrors, using several sets of information to take appropriate action. The ways in which children explore print as they write and as they read somehow seem to give the young learner a better overview of the complexity of language in print. Some detail that has caught the child's attention turns up again in a different kind of situation.

Beginning writing in school

Practice varies from education system to education system: some prefer children to write on blank pages and teachers watch as children gradually bring directional behaviours under control. In other education systems teachers are firmly convinced that paper with horizontal lines helps children, making it easier to learn to work in an ordered way across a page. The requirement for the two writing tasks in the Observation Survey is a standard one. For these assessments one of the individual differences we need to learn about is what the child already does or does not know about putting print onto a page. Therefore the standard situation is to use a blank page, which will reveal greater variance among the children about their control of writing; and that is precisely what we are trying to find out — who varies and in what way. What is done in a teaching situation is still a matter for teachers and systems to decide.

The developmental arguments for the 'blank page' decision in the assessment situation are provided in Chapter 2.

Rating technique for early writing

Rating techniques can be used on children's early attempts to write stories. For example, to rate writing *in the first year of school* take three samples of the child's stories on consecutive days or over a couple of weeks. (One sample is not sufficiently reliable for this evaluation technique.) Rate them for language level, message quality and directional principles. Summarise the progress as satisfactory or unsatisfactory using the table below.

Language level
Record the number of the highest level of linguistic organisation used by the child:

1   alphabetical (letters only)
2   or word (any recognisable word)
3   or word group (any two-word phrase)
4   or sentence (any simple sentence)
5   or punctuated story (of two or more sentences)
6   or paragraphed story (two themes).

Message quality
Record the number for the best description of the child's sample:

1   he has a concept of signs (uses letters, invents letters, uses punctuation)
2   or he has a concept that a message is conveyed
3   or a message is copied
4   or he makes repetitive use of sentence patterns such as 'Here is a …'
5   or attempts to record his own ideas
6   or he produces successful composition.

Directional principles
Record the number of the highest rating for which there is no error in the sample of the child's writing:

1   no evidence of directional knowledge
2   or part of the directional pattern is known: start top left, or move left to right, or return down left
3   or reversal of the directional pattern (right to left and return down right)
4   or correct directional pattern
5   or correct directional pattern and spaces between words
6   or extensive text without any difficulties of arrangement and spacing of text.

	A Language Level	B Message Quality	C Directional Principles
Not yet satisfactory	1 – 4	1 – 4	1 – 4
Probably satisfactory	5 – 6	5 – 6	5 – 6

> One child's writing after two weeks in school:
>
> † rɪ ɛrɪf

> The same child's writing after 12 weeks:
>
> I went to
> blankets FeLL bed off and my me.

Sometimes what children learn falls outside the limits of the analysis categories that teachers use. Michael was five and in his first year of school, but at home he had access to his father's computer. Unaided he 'pecked out' this story on the keyboard, bypassing the need to form letters.

> Mr. snowe by michael.
>
> wun cod and snowee morning
>
> a boy came out to plae
>
> and he made a snoe man
>
> and when it was nite time
>
> farethe cris mis came too visit adlaide.

The story combines local knowledge (of Adelaide, Australia) with story knowledge about 'snowee' mornings and snowmen, which rarely occur in Adelaide, and with fantasy knowledge about 'farethe cris mis'.

It is part of the fun of making careful observations of children who are writing that we can reflect on how they draw from diverse sources of knowledge as they construct their stories.

Writing Vocabulary task

I observed the writing of 100 children once every week in a research study. One thing I noticed was that the more competent children made lists of all the words they knew. These lists of words are interesting. Mark's list in English and Erena's list in Maori (Rau, 1998), written when they were 5 years and 11 months and 5 years 5 months respectively, were both produced spontaneously at home.

Examine Mark's list. Assuming that he was writing down the page, notice how a word he has just written seems to suggest another word he might write. Mark found words that started the same (It, is, in), that ended the same (at, bat, hat), that were opposites (come, go), that form a category of family names (Mum, Dad, Mark, Denise), that are the same but different (car, cat, bell, ball) and so on.

From observations like these Sara M. Robinson (1973) devised a useful observation task which has all the properties of a good test when it is used in the first two years of

Mark's list

Erena's list

(Rau, 1998)

school. Robinson's writing vocabulary task is like a screen upon which the child can project what he knows — not only what we have taught him but what he has learned anywhere in his various worlds. The child samples his own universe of knowledge. This is appropriate because when learners are near the beginning of learning in a new field the kind of sampling of knowledge used in test construction does not work — what you are sampling is in very short supply. There is not enough common knowledge among beginners to use a sampling approach.

A task was constructed where the child was encouraged to write down all the words he knew how to write, starting with his own name and making a personal list of words he had managed to learn. This simple test was reliable (that is, a child tended to score at a similar level when retested within two weeks) and had a high relationship with reading words in isolation. Even before he begins formal literacy instruction a child can respond to the instruction 'Write all the words you know.' How children respond changes over time, and highly competent children can demonstrate long lists of words even after a limited time at school.

This is an assessment that a teacher can do in any place at any time, needing nothing but her personal knowledge of how to make such observations and scoring them in systematic ways.

Although some children will write nothing or just the first letter of their name, other young children will write more than 40–45 words in 10 minutes, the time allowed for this observation. This provides a score which correlates well with other literacy measures and changes over time, and has good measurement qualities. When the child can write more than 40–45 words the value of this score for predicting future changes in literacy learning diminishes. After that the teacher can begin to measure how the child works with a more traditional spelling or writing task.

So, like many observation tasks, this one is very useful for a short period of time (about one to two years), telling us how fast a child is building control over a basic writing vocabulary.

Once formal schooling begins, the distribution of scores on this observation task changes markedly with age. This is shown in the stanine tables, as the raw scores for, say, Stanine 5, change across age groups (page 109).

Writing Vocabulary scores are very sensitive to the instructional procedures of the classroom. High scores will be associated with very different programmes which (a) foster early writing or (b) place an emphasis on word learning. Low scores will be associated with programmes that provide few opportunities for children to write or encourage writing but expect only invented spellings.

In the first year of school there is probably a high degree of interdependence between reading words and writing words, but it should not be assumed that reading success in the first years of learning would be assured simply by teaching children to write words.

Using the Writing Vocabulary observation task

Administration

The child is allowed 10 minutes to complete this task. Give the child a pen or pencil and a copy of the observation sheet (page 111) with the top folded under.

To introduce the task, say to the child:

- *I want to see how many words you can write.*
  Can you write your name?

(Start the 10-minute timing here.)

If the child says 'No' see if he knows any single-letter or two-letter words. Say:

- *Do you know how to write 'is' (pause), 'to' (pause), 'I' (pause)?*
  and then suggest other words that he may know (see below), pausing between each word for the child's response.

If the child says 'Yes' say:

- *Write your name for me.*

  When the child finishes say:

- *Good. Now think of all the words you know how to write and write them all down.*

  When he stops writing, or when he needs prompting, suggest words that he might know how to write, pausing between each word for the child's response.

- *Do you know how to write 'go' (pause), 'me' (pause)?*

- *Do you know how to write 'look' (pause), 'come' (pause)?*

Select words that the child might have met in his reading books or might be able to work out how to write; use some of the following words to get the writing under way.

```
I    a   is   in   am   to   come   like   see   the   my   we   and   at
here  on  up   look  go   this   it   me
           (This is not a list to be dictated or used for teaching!)
```

Continue for 10 minutes or until the child's writing vocabulary is exhausted. Prompt the child as much as you like with words he might be able to write. Be careful not to interfere with his thinking and his searching of his own repertoire.

The child should not be asked to read the words he has written.

Very able children need little prompting. Sometimes it is necessary to suggest a category of words but do not prompt for words in a series. To focus children's attention on other words a good open-ended question is:

Do you know any other words like that?

To shift the child's attention to other words and contexts a few of these questions might be used.

Do you know how to write any children's names?
Do you know how to write things you do?
Do you know how to write about things in your house?
Do you know how to write about things you eat?
Do you know how to write …?

Recording and scoring

Correct spelling: Each completed word scores one point if it is correctly spelled:

- but not if the child accidentally writes a word that is correct but spontaneously tells you that it is another word. For example, he writes 'am' and says without prompting that it is 'on'

- and not when the observer realises from some other evidence that the child does not know what word he has written.

Reversed letters: The formation of individual letters (including the reversal of letters) does not influence the scoring except when the letter form represents a different letter. So, words with one or more reversed letters are correct when the intended letters are clear (for example 'buꙅ' for 'bus'). They are not correct if the reversed letter could be a different letter (for example 'qop' for 'pop') and they are not correct if the intended letters are not clear (e.g. reversed 'e' looks like 'g', or 'run' that looks like 'nun').

Words written right to left: These are scored as correct only if the child actually wrote the letters from right to left. Individual letters may or may not be reversed ('nac' for 'can') which means that words scored as correct may have a mixture of reversed and correctly oriented letters.

Series of words: Teachers should not prompt for words in series, or in a rhyming set or a spelling pattern group like 'sat, fat, mat, hat'. However, when children spontaneously produce a series of words like 'look, looks, looking' or 'sat, fat, mat', each word is counted.

Capital letters: Capital letters are acceptable substitutions for lower case letters and vice versa. Therefore the word 'I' written as 'i' is scored as correct.

Stanine scores

To compare the child's performance with that of other children use one of the tables of scores below. In this book each task has four age tables. Select the table which will allow you to compare the child's score with those of other children of his age (see page 126). Look up the total raw score obtained by the child you assessed on the age table that is right for him and read from the second line of boxes his scaled score, a number between 1 and 9. This scaled score is called a stanine and it provides a guide to how well the child compares with a sample of 796 New Zealand children in February 2000. If the score on the table is allocated across more than one stanine group choose the lowest value: that is, be conservative rather than generous.

WRITING VOCABULARY STANINES FOR FOUR AGE GROUPS

Writing Vocabulary: 5.00 – 5.50 years
(N = 223; Score Range: 0–130; Mean = 12.9; SE = 0.89; SD = 13.4)

Test Score	0	1	2–3	4–6	7–11	12–18	19–32	33–48	49+
Stanine Grp	1	2	3	4	5	6	7	8	9

Writing Vocabulary: 5.51 – 6.00 years
(N = 170; Score Range: 0–130; Mean = 23.8; SE = 1.33; SD = 17.4)

Test Score	0–2	3–5	6–8	9–15	16–26	27–37	38–48	49–58	59+
Stanine Grp	1	2	3	4	5	6	7	8	9

Writing Vocabulary: 6.01 – 6.50 years
(N = 230; Score Range: 0–130; Mean = 42.7; SE = 1.51; SD = 22.9)

Test Score	0–4	5–13	14–25	26–36	37–49	50–59	60–69	70–83	84+
Stanine Grp	1	2	3	4	5	6	7	8	9

Writing Vocabulary: 6.51 – 7.00 years
(N = 173; Score Range: 0–130; Mean = 51.0; SE = 1.69; SD = 22.3)

Test Score	0–8	9–25	26–35	36–45	46–56	57–66	67–80	81–99	100+
Stanine Grp	1	2	3	4	5	6	7	8	9

(For more technical information see Appendices.)

Immediately preceding the summary of the Observation Survey results (Chapter 10, pages 126–128), readers will find a general discussion of stanine scores, why they are used, when they are helpful and what their limitations are. (See pages 155–160 for stanine scores for Canada, the United Kingdom and the United States.)

Interpreting Writing Vocabulary scores

A poor writing vocabulary may indicate that, despite all his efforts to read, a child is in fact taking very little notice of the visual differences in print. He requires an all-out teaching effort and a great deal of help to elicit early writing behaviours. In this learning the hand and eye support and supplement each other. Only later does the eye become the solo agent and learning becomes faster than in the eye-plus-hand learning stage (Clay, 1991).

Many kinds of experiences, in school and out of school, with letters, numbers, words, stories, drawing and life in the real world have enabled the child to learn many things about print such as where it is used and what kinds of things it can tell us. Despite a high degree of interdependence between reading and writing words, they are not necessarily linked. Some research has looked closely at words children can spell which they cannot read. Some children cannot read words that they can write, and vice versa. However, instructional programmes vary in the extent to which they allow or foster this reciprocity.

Keeping records of writing progress

A record of a child's progress may be kept in one of the following ways.

An inventory of writing vocabulary
If the writing observation is done at several points of time — at entry, after six months and after one year — this provides one type of record of change over time in early writing. In this example the progress of a child called Marc is clear from the record itself without any reference to scores or stanines.

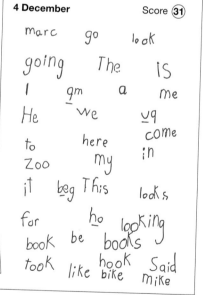

Marc — writing vocabulary

Record change over time in daily or weekly writing
A teacher can keep a list of new words written independently by certain students to whom she is currently paying particular attention (see Writing Vocabulary Weekly Record Sheet, page 112).

WRITING VOCABULARY OBSERVATION SHEET

Date: _____

Name: _____ Age: _____

Recorder: _____ Date of Birth: _____

TEST SCORE: ☐

STANINE GROUP: ☐

(Fold heading under before child uses sheet)

- -

COMMENTS

WRITING VOCABULARY WEEKLY RECORD SHEET

Name: _____

Date of Birth: _____

Initial Testing: Date:	Week: Date:	Week: Date:	Week: Date:	Week: Date:
Week: Date:	Week: Date:	Week: Date:	Week: Date:	Week: Date:

An accumulated Writing Vocabulary chart

The teacher could make a graph of the accumulated totals on the weekly record sheet. To start the record for Week 1 enter the number of words written correctly on the initial Writing Vocabulary observation task. Then each week add, cumulatively, the number of new words the child writes independently in the stories he is writing in the classroom. A cumulative record of writing vocabulary is a sensitive reflection of the child's increasing control over writing, and it is a reliable indicator of slow progress. Alternatively, a teacher might plot the results of several successive Writing Vocabulary tasks (see below).

Change over time in Writing Vocabulary scores

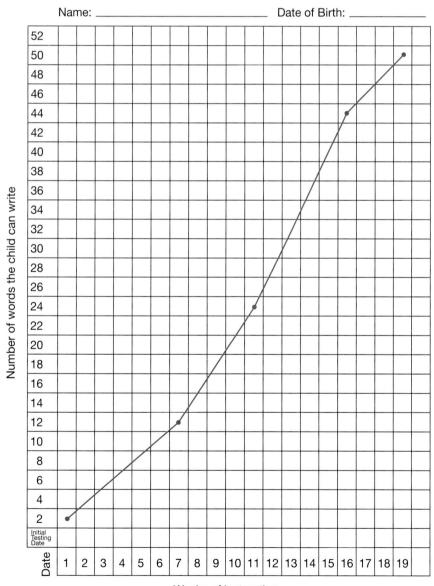

Running records of writing progress

It is surprisingly difficult to take running records of a young child writing with the teacher's assistance. In a classroom the teacher is either interacting with the child or allowing the child to interact with informed others who help the child as he writes. In several research studies students have tried to devise ways of recording what occurs in such observations but it turns out to be much more difficult than taking running records of reading.

In order to capture children's behaviour while writing in their classrooms during the first four years of school a running record of writing behaviour was developed (Boocock, 1991). Each child's stream of behaviour during five minutes of their writing time was recorded or coded as it occurred onto a complex grid of predefined categories to capture oral, written and other behaviours. Experienced observers of reading behaviour found it challenging to record all writing behaviour. Most difficult to capture were the oral responses of the children before, during and after the observation (Boocock, McNaughton and Parr, 1998).

In a report which appeared in *The Reading Teacher* there is a record which traces a child's progress in the first 10 weeks of school. That record had to be simplified leaving out many things that the observer saw. In that record it is possible to show the child becoming a more independent writer in a few weeks. It is also an interesting account of what the teacher was trying to achieve as she worked alongside the child (Girling-Butcher, Phillips and Clay, 1991).

Those who wish to take observation records of children writing in authentic situations in interaction with teachers, children or other helpers should be warned to be ready for complicated sequences of behaviour.

An older child who can write 50 or more words is too competent for the Writing Vocabulary task to be a satisfactory assessment of writing competence. The child should be encouraged to write a story of several sentences or paragraphs (with as little help as possible) to provide a basis for grouping or categorising children's stories according to selected criteria. To assess change over time an earlier record for one child can be compared with a later one and the progress made should be clearly articulated. Kay has reached this transition point: her writing will be evaluated by changes in writing continuous text in the future.

Here is a house Said Betty. Yes Said Paul. Yes Said Ben. I said yes, too. Ben said it is a blue house. Yes said Betty. Yes said Paul. I said yes two

Older children can be given a spelling test which usually yields some kind of standard test score. Spelling tests are often constructed with particular sets of words — regular words, irregular words, spelling 'demons', Greek roots, and so on. Such constraints must be taken into account when interpreting the child's observed behaviour, and such behaviour should not be generalised to the writing of words outside the set of words used in the observation task.

Another kind of test of spelling is to ask children to proof-read: that is, to find the misspelled words.

Useful information from spelling observations is the evidence that is provided by watching the child at work and noting his strengths (words known, ways of getting to new words that work, analogies that are tried). After the child has reached the upper threshold of his spelling achievement (where mostly correct spelling passes over to too much incorrect spelling) the incorrect responses provide evidence of risk-taking, control of spelling patterns, the use of analogy, the rule-guided behaviour, and also of gaps, confusions or unproductive actions.

9 Observation task for Hearing and Recording Sounds in Words

Hearing and Recording Sounds in Words

Going from phonemic awareness to letter-sound relationships

At first this observation task was called dictation because the teacher asks the child to record a dictated sentence. But the child's product is scored by counting the child's representation of the sounds (phonemes) by letters (graphemes). Being able to hear the sounds in the words you want to write is an authentic task — a task one encounters in the real world rather than one devised merely for the purpose of assessing. It calls upon the writer to listen to the sounds in words in sequence and to find letters to represent those sounds.

This observation task has directed the attention of teachers and children to phonemic awareness since its development in 1977, and it fits very well into the emphasis in the research literature on phonemic awareness. It arose not from the experimental studies of the 1980s but from the descriptive studies of the 1970s (Chomsky, 1972; Elkonin in Downing, 1973; Read, 1975; Clay, 1979a).

School entrants can speak a language and need to learn to read and write it. They need to work out how every aspect of their spoken language relates to messages in print. Children need to learn how the language knowledge they already have can help them to read and write messages. One of the things they already know is how to use most of the sounds of their language. (There are a few sounds in English which 20–30 percent of five-year-olds find difficult to hear and say. See Clay, 1966.)

Recent research has made it clear that we must pay attention to four aspects of how the sounds of English are represented in print.

- Children have to learn to hear the sounds buried within words, and this is not an easy task.

- Children have to learn to visually discriminate the symbols we use in print, and this is a large set of symbols. (See examples on pages 84 and 85.)

- Children have to learn to link single symbols and clusters of symbols with the sounds they represent.

- Children have to learn that there are many alternatives and exceptions in our system of putting sounds into print.

Long before they have learned all there is to know about letters and sounds children begin to work on relationships among a few things which they have learned. You do not have to know all the members of a set before you can work out some of the set's characteristics. Also, while some teachers are tediously teaching one letter-sound link after another in reading or writing, some children have already begun to read or write using bigger chunks of information.

- It is more efficient to work with larger chunks, and so they do!

- Sometimes it is more efficient to work with relationships (like some word I know) rather than items of knowledge (like letters), and so they do!

- Often it is efficient to use a vague sense of a rule, and so they do!

They do not wait for the teacher to get through all her lessons on sounds before they begin working with larger chunks and relationships.

Using the Hearing and Recording Sounds in Words observation task

Hearing and recording sounds in words is a useful observation task to capture the child's control of sound-to-letter links. The teacher tells the child a sentence to be written. The child is encouraged to write what he can hear in the words dictated. What he does not hear will not get recorded. Scores show how successful the child was at hearing the sounds in the words and finding a possible way of recording those sounds in English spelling. (The task is not a pure assessment of phonemic awareness because what the child has learned about spelling, or orthography, may also turn up in his recording.)

The child is given credit for every phoneme (sound) that he writes correctly, even though the whole word may not be correctly spelt. The scores give some indication of the child's ability 1) to analyse the word he hears or says and 2) to find a way of recording in letters the sounds that he can hear. The children's scores change over time from low to high as they become more competent at this kind of task.

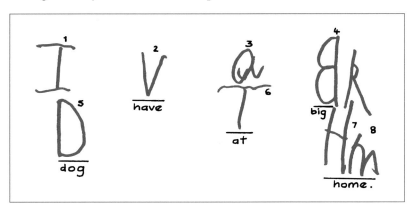

Administration

The observer selects one of five alternative sentences to use in this observation. To avoid a practice effect use one of the five alternative forms for an initial assessment and another alternative form for a subsequent reassessment.

Form A	I have a big dog at home. Today I am going to take him to school.
Form B	Mum/Mom has gone up to the shop. She will get milk and bread.
Form C	I can see the red boat that we are going to have a ride in.
Form D	The bus is coming. It will stop here to let me get on.
Form E	The boy is riding his bike. He can go very fast on it.

Give the child a pen or pencil and a copy of the observation sheet on page 124 with the top folded under.

To introduce the task say to the child:
- *I am going to read you a story. When I have read it through once I will read it again very slowly so that you can write down the words in the story.*

Read the test sentence to the child at normal speed. Then say:
- *Some of the words are hard. Say them slowly and think how you can write them.*
- *Start writing the words now.*

Dictate slowly, word by word. When the child comes to a problem word say:
- *You say it slowly. How would you start to write it?*
- *What can you hear?*

Then add:
- *What else can you hear?*

If the child cannot complete the word say:
- *We'll leave that word. The next one is …*

Point to where to write the next word if this helps the child.

Support the child with comments like those above to keep the child working at the task.

Recording and scoring

Write the text below the child's version after the task is finished.

hm	skol	b
him	school	big

Rules for scoring are necessary to ensure reliability and validity when the task is used for measurement of progress or change. Check with the scoring standard for the form you selected (A, B, C, D or E — see page 121).

While initially the child's progress will be in the area of 'hearing and recording sounds in words', as he moves towards more control over writing we must expect him to be learning something about the orthography (the spelling rules and patterns) of the language.

Score one point for each phoneme the child has analysed and recorded that is numbered 1 to 37 on the examples (page 121), and record the total out of 37.

There can be no set of rules for scoring that will cover the ingenuity found in children's attempts. Scorers are advised to be conservative rather than liberal in applying the following scoring criteria if comparable results are to be achieved across different scorers.

The teacher who is a sensitive observer would note any partially correct responses which tell a great deal about the cutting edge of the child's knowledge. Such qualitative information is very important for planning the kind of help to offer the child.

(I am very aware of the arguments about developmental change from partially correct to correct responding. However, recorders do not agree on how to score partially correct responding and so for a reliable measuring instrument only the correct responding criteria for scoring can be recommended.)

Additions, omissions and letters produced in an unusual order

If a letter does not have a number underneath it in the scoring standards on page 121, then it receives no score (even if a preceding letter has been omitted). Additions do not affect scoring as long as numbered letters are included.

tody	Score 3	todae	Score 4	stop	Score 4
today		today		1st 2nd 4th 3rd	

Capital letters

Capital letters are acceptable substitutions for lower case letters and vice versa.

Substitutions

Given what is being observed in this task it makes sense to accept a response when the sound analysis has been a useful one, even though the child has used letters which can record the sound but in this particular case the spelling is incorrect.

As a general principle substitute letters are acceptable if, in English, the sound is sometimes recorded in that way. Consonant substitutions which count as correct are those like 'k' and 'c', and 's' and 'c':

skool	tace	cee	c
school	take	see	see

and vowel substitutions which count as correct are:

cum	cuming	caming	bak	bas
come	coming	coming	bake	bus

where the indefinite article 'a' is a word pronounced like the 'u' in 'bus'.

As children try to analyse the sounds in vowels they are likely to substitute unusual analyses of diphthongs. Here is a substitution which does not alter the scoring.

todae
today

Children may even replace one vowel with a letter that represents a vowel made in a neighbouring area of the mouth. No credit is given for using 'a' for 'e'.

vare
very

1 23

It may seem arbitrary to some readers but given that the children are reading English I would score the 'e' for 'y' substitution as acceptable and the 'a' for 'e' substitution as unacceptable, in the immediately preceding example. If you disagree with me a different scoring would make little difference to the overall score.

Changes in letter order

Where the child has made a change in letter order take one mark off for that word. For example:

ma	$2 - 1 = 1$		gonig	$5 - 1 = 4$
am			going	

Alternative sentences for Hearing and Recording Sounds in Words with Scoring Standards

Select one of the following alternative forms: A, B, C, D or E.

Form A I have a big dog at home.
1   2 3 4   5   6 7 8   9 10 11   12 13   14 15 16

Today I am going to take him
17 18 19 20   21 22   23 24 25 26 27   28 29 30   31 32 33

to sc h oo l.
34 35   36 37

Form B M u m/Mom has gone up to the sh o p.
1 2 3   4 5 6   7 8 9   10 11   12 13   14 15   16 17 18

She will get milk and
19 20   21 22 23   24 25 26   27 28 29 30   31 32 33

bread.
34 35 36   37

Form C I can see the red
1   2 3 4   5 6   7 8   9 10 11

boat that we are going
12 13 14   15 16 17   18 19   20 21   22 23 24 25 26

to have a ride in.
27 28   29 30 31   32   33 34 35   36 37

Form D The bus is coming. It
1 2   3 4 5   6 7   8 9 10 11 12 13   14 15

will stop here to let me
16 17 18   19 20 21 22   23 24 25   26 27   28 29 30   31 32

get on.
33 34 35   36 37

Form E The boy is riding his bike.
1 2   3 4   5 6   7 8 9 10 11 12   13 14 15   16 17 18

He can go very fast on it.
19 20   21 22 23   24 25   26 27 28 29   30 31 32 33   34 35   36 37

Reversed letters

Reversed letters are not correct if they could represent a different letter. Another criterion that can be used is that if the letter used never makes the sound(s) being recorded, the substitutions used count as errors, as in:

$$\frac{\text{dig}}{\text{big}} \qquad \frac{\text{bog}}{\text{dog}}$$

Some special problems

- In Form A: Only score the word 'I' once. Score the word 'to' once; either in 'today' or in 'to'.

- In Form B: The final phoneme in 'has' is /z/: credit either 's' or 'z'.

- In Form C: There are only two phonemes to score in 'see'.

- In any form: 'th' and 'sh' score 1 for both letters and 0 for only one letter.

- 'ng' is scored as two phonemes. It enables equal scoring of 37 in each of the alternative sentences while also recognising variable pronunciation in different speech communities.

Making notes on other observations

It is important that the observer also make notes on the following:

- any sequencing errors

- the omission of sounds

- unusual placement of letters within words

- partially correct attempts

- and 'good' confusions.

Any of these may tell the teacher something about what the learner knows and how the teacher may support some shift in performance.

Score according to the scoring standards, calculate the total, and consult the stanine table for the appropriate age group.

Stanine scores

To compare the child's performance with that of other children use one of the tables of scores on page 123. In this book each task has four age tables. Select the table which will allow you to compare the child's score with those of other children of his age (see page 126). Look up the total raw score obtained by the child you assessed on the age table that is right for him and read from the second line of boxes his scaled score, a number between 1 and 9. This scaled score is called a stanine and it provides a guide to how well the child compares with a sample of 796 New Zealand children in February 2000. If the score on the table is allocated across more than one stanine group choose the lowest value: that is, be conservative rather than generous.

Immediately preceding the summary of the Observation Survey results (Chapter 10, pages 126–128), readers will find a general discussion of stanine scores, why they are used, when they are helpful and what their limitations are. (See pages 155–160 for stanine scores for Canada, the United Kingdom and the United States.)

One would expect children to completely master this learning and move through the stanine score range until they reach near-perfect scoring. Slips and measurement errors may be responsible for less than perfect scores. Every score you calculate will be surrounded by a band of potential measurement error (see 'SE' below).

HEARING AND RECORDING SOUNDS IN WORDS STANINES FOR FOUR AGE GROUPS

Hearing and Recording Sounds in Words: 5.00 – 5.50 years
(N = 223; Score Range: 0–37; Mean = 15.6; SE = 0.77; SD = 11.6)

Test Score	0	1	2–4	5–11	12–18	19–26	27–33	34–36	37
Stanine Grp	1	2	3	4	5	6	7	8	9

Hearing and Recording Sounds in Words: 5.51 – 6.00 years
(N = 170; Score Range: 0–37; Mean = 23.6; SE = 0.81; SD = 10.5)

Test Score	0–1	2–7	8–15	16–22	23–29	30–33	34–36	– 37 –	
Stanine Grp	1	2	3	4	5	6	7	8	9

Hearing and Recording Sounds in Words: 6.01 – 6.50 years
(N = 230; Score Range: 0–37; Mean = 30.7; SE = 0.56; SD = 8.4)

Test Score	0–8	9–19	20–27	28–32	33–35	36	– – – 37 – – –		
Stanine Grp	1	2	3	4	5	6	7	8	9

Hearing and Recording Sounds in Words: 6.51 – 7.00 years
(N = 173; Score Range: 0–37; Mean = 33.2; SE = 0.49; SD = 6.5)

Test Score	0–14	15–28	29–32	33–35	36	– – – – 37 – – – –			
Stanine Grp	1	2	3	4	5	6	7	8	9

(For more technical information see Appendices.)

HEARING AND RECORDING SOUNDS IN WORDS
OBSERVATION SHEET

Date: _____

Name: _____ Age: _____

Recorder: _____ Date of Birth: _____

TEST SCORE: [/37]

STANINE GROUP: [   ]

(Fold heading under before child uses sheet)

COMMENTS

Interpreting the Hearing and Recording Sounds in Words observation task

Observing change over time

Sara Robinson and Barbara Watson devised and used the Hearing and Recording Sounds in Words forms A–E during the development of Reading Recovery. The task proved to be a valuable indicator of change over time of a child's ability to go from his analysis of sounds in spoken words to written forms for representing these sounds. In that sense this is neither a dictation nor a spelling test.

In the following example a teacher, who would normally use an alternative form when reassessing a child, has used Form A for both an early and a later assessment in order to demonstrate to the reader how well the assessment has captured the changes which occurred.

Timothy scored quite well on Hearing Sounds in Words. In February he recorded 19 phonemes out of 37. Five months later when he was reassessed he had a score of 30.

Timothy's record

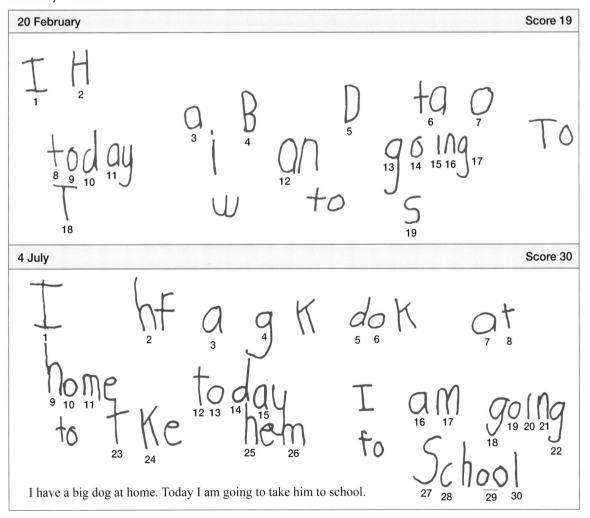

10 Summarising the Observation Survey results

Change over time in early literacy learning

In the summary of the Observation Survey the teacher brings together what she has observed. Before describing useful ways to integrate these results some discussion of the use of stanines and percentiles is necessary.

The tables for the observation tasks in this book allow teachers to obtain a raw score for each task and then to make a comparison between the child who has been assessed and a large representative sample of New Zealand children of similar age obtained in the year 2000. There are four age tables. The shift to the next age table is made on the child's birthday or exactly six months later.

Stanines are scores which redistribute raw scores according to a normal curve in nine groups from 1 (a low score) to 9 (a high score) (see Lyman, 1963). They are normalised standard scores. When you place a child in a stanine group you have placed the child in a 'temporary progress category'. You should not do *arithmetic* with these categories. The Observation Survey stanines should not be summed or averaged, for example, when selecting children for a placement.

The temporary progress categories formed by each range of stanines suggest that:

- the child in the 4–6 range should find himself able to participate in the average classroom activities

- the child in the 7–9 range is probably eager to reach out to more complex or challenging tasks

- the child in the 3–4 range is already struggling with average tasks in the class and needs extra teacher attention if this situation is to be changed

- the child in the 0–2 range is unlikely to be able to 'catch up' without immediate, intensive, expert teaching.

Stanines are particularly useful for quite a different reason. It makes no sense to compare the raw scores of a child across the survey tasks because each task has a different total score. Stanines can be used to compare a pupil's scores across the various tasks because all the scores are placed on the same measuring scale, from 1 to 9. A pupil's scores can be compared on several quite different types of observations, and knowing the highs and lows of a pupil's performance profile can help with the planning of instruction.

Where a raw score value on the table is allocated across more than one stanine choose the lowest stanine value: that is, be conservative rather than generous.

Where a stanine score on the table is allocated across more than one raw score value, also be conservative rather than generous in your appraisal. Think of the child as just getting into the lower group.

On these tasks most children move from low scores on entry to school to high scores after one to two years at school, and it is desirable for all children to get close to perfect scores for the letters of the alphabet, the sound-letter relationships task (HRSW), and the short word reading task designed for beginning readers.

When we are assessing something in which we expect children to eventually reach perfect scoring (as in Letter Identification, Concepts About Print and Word Reading) we must expect older children to begin to cluster on the high scores. The higher the achievement in a particular cluster of schools the lower will be the maximum stanine that can be achieved on that task. For teaching purposes the raw scores will then be most informative, for the questions by that time are 'How close is the child to knowing all the letters (perfect scoring)?' and 'Which few items must we work on?'

When the child is reassessed it is likely that a different age table will be used because the child is older. We are still comparing the child with his peers of the same age. On this second assessment the child's stanine category may be higher, the same, or lower. If it is the same the child is maintaining his position relative to his age peers. If it is higher the child is gaining on his peers and closing any previous gap. If it is lower, the child's peers are pushing ahead at a faster rate than this child is learning.

There may be a good reason for a school, a district, or a particular community group to build up its own table of stanine scores. Teachers could accumulate data over several years against which to compare individual children, or each year's intake of children on this aspect of literacy learning. A professional in tests and measurement could assist with this.

For the use of researchers two other kinds of data are provided in the appendices. For comparison purposes percentile ranks for each of the age groups in the normative population are provided for five tasks. Many teachers find stanines a useful way to think of how a child relates to his age peers. Research statisticians assure us that percentiles have better measurement qualities than the stanines have when the achievement distributions are changing over time.

Teachers find stanines within a limited age range useful when they need to evaluate individual children for instruction or placement.

Another set of interesting information is provided in the charts which show how markedly the distributions of scores change over time as the children move through the first two years of school. Hopefully the presentation of these data will allow practitioners, theorists and researchers to design instruction and research which takes into account the shape of the distributions of scores, and the marked changes that occur across these two years. Of particular interest is the fact that learning seems to spurt and slow at different times in different task areas. What is critical for schools is to be able to identify who remains in the lowest achieving group when all this change has taken place, and to provide intensive help for those children who would, without it, face many new educational challenges in the next ten years of schooling.

Teachers should decide for which children they need a full analysis of the Observation Survey. They may, for example:

- make notes on teaching points for competent children

- make brief summaries for a broad average group

- produce detailed write-ups for children whose progress really puzzles them.

They will be able to describe what the child can do, and also what is partially known, at the boundaries of the child's knowledge.

Making a summary of the Observation Survey results

The Observation Survey provides detailed information. A first step towards an integrative summary is to bring the results together under a list of headings. (See the two Observation Survey Summary Sheets which follow, on page 130 and page 132.)

Text reading and other observation tasks

On Side 1 of the Observation Summary Sheet (page 130) transfer the detail from the Running Records obtained at three levels: the analysis of the kinds of information the child was using and neglecting to use when processing the information in print, and the statements about how the reading sounded. Then record the results from the other observation tasks on the lower half of Side 1.

Think about strategic activity (processing)

There are several reasons for this detailed approach to summarising the Observation Survey results on Side 2 of the Summary Sheet (pages 132 and 137).

- A language is organised hierarchically on several levels. Only three levels have been selected here: text (a general term to stand for phrase, sentence or larger text), word level, and letter level.

- It has been argued (Clay, 1991) that although the reader appears to have stored many items of knowledge in memory he has also learned ways of working with the information in print — ways of finding it, storing it, filing it, retrieving it, and linking or cross-referencing one kind of information with another kind.

Good observation, rather than modern linguistic theory, led talented reading clinician Grace Fernald (1943) to formulate these two statements about the relationships of letters, words and texts in reading.

- Groups of words must be the focus of attention in reading. Attending to the words as separate units, as in word-by-word reading, loses important meanings. The meaning of a word can vary with the group in which it occurs or, in another way, a group of words has a certain meaning. The sentence is the context within which the meaning of the word group is confirmed. The known word is the unit at which level the precision of the word group is usually confirmed.

- For the unknown, unfamiliar, forgotten or misperceived word the reader's attention must go to clusters of letters or even to individual letters but whether these are right or not must be confirmed at the level of the word unit.

She insisted therefore that, in writing, the word should always be written as a unit, and in reading, words should always be used in context.

A guide to analysing the child's problem-solving (processing of print)

On Side 2 of the Observation Survey Summary Sheet make an analysis of the ways in which the child identifies and solves problems or new challenges. Complete each section under useful and problem strategic activity (1) on text, (2) with words, and (3) with letters. Use the questions on pages 133–135 to help you. Some examples of what is meant by strategic activity are given in the completed record for Chris (page 137).

Comments should be made on the child's performance in relation to each of the following six topics.

- Useful strategic activity on text reading.

- Problem strategic activity on text reading.

- Useful strategic activity with words.

- Problem strategic activity with words.

- Useful strategic activity with letters and sounds, separately and in clusters.

- Problem strategic activity with letters and sounds, separately and in clusters.

OBSERVATION SURVEY SUMMARY SHEET

Name: _____ Date: _____ D. of B.: _____ Age: _____ yrs _____ mths

School: _____ Recorder: _____

Text Titles		Errors Running Words	Error Ratio	Accuracy Rate	Self-correction Ratio
Easy	_____	_____	1: _____	_____ %	1: _____
Instructional	_____	_____	1: _____	_____ %	1: _____
Hard	_____	_____	1: _____	_____ %	1: _____

Directional movement _____

Analysis of Errors and Self-corrections
Information used or neglected [Meaning (M), Structure or Syntax (S), Visual (V)]

Easy _____

Instructional _____

_____

Hard _____

_____

Cross-checking on information (Note that this behaviour changes over time)

_____

			Raw Score	Stanine
How the reading sounds	**Easy** **Instructional** **Hard**			
Letter Identi-fication				
Concepts About Print	* **Sand** **Stones** **Shoes** **Moon**			
Word Reading	* **List A** **List B** **List C** **Other** _____ (Enter test name)			
Writing Vocabulary				
Hearing and Recording Sounds in Words	* **A** **B** **C** **D** **E**			
Other tasks	**Writing sample** **Story**			

* Circle whatever was used

OBSERVATION SURVEY SUMMARY SHEET

Name: __Chris__   Date: __8.6.11__   D. of B.: __5.5.05__   Age: __6__ yrs __1__ mths

School: __Ferndale__   Recorder: __MM__

Text Titles		Errors Running Words	Error Ratio	Accuracy Rate	Self-correction Ratio
Easy	Sam's Mask (RTR) (S)	$\frac{0}{41}$	1: —	100 %	1: 1
Instructional	Baby Lamb's First Drink (PM) (S)	$\frac{6}{64}$	1: 10.7	90 %	1: —
Hard	Blackberries (PM) (S)	$\frac{21}{108}$	1: 5.1	80 %	1: 22

Directional movement   Pointing on only 3 pages across all texts.

Analysis of Errors and Self-corrections
Information used or neglected [Meaning (M), Structure or Syntax (S), Visual (V)]

Easy   Appears to be led by meaning and structure.

Instructional   Errors show use of meaning and structure with visual information overlooked in most instances.

Hard   Used meaning and structure consistently, with some use of visual information. Self-corrected by using visual information.

Cross-checking on information (Note that this behaviour changes over time)
One clear example of the use of visual information to cross-check with meaning and structure on the hard text.

How the reading sounds	Easy	Read slowly and carefully word by word.		
	Instructional	Careful reading with a little intonation.		
	Hard	Slow reading with some intonation but little phrasing.		

			Raw Score	Stanine
Letter Identi-fic ation	Mainly alphabet name response. Some confusions with letters that look similar: $\frac{q}{p}$ $\frac{p}{b}$ $\frac{n}{h}$ $\frac{i}{l}$ $\frac{p}{q}$ Other confusions: $\frac{x}{z}$ $\frac{Q}{Y}$ $\frac{8}{g}$ Letter unknown: y		44	2
Concepts About Print	* Sand (Stones) Shoes Moon	Knows print contains a message, controls directional movement, first and last concepts and meaning of a full stop (period). Identifies letters appropriately.	10	1
Word Reading	* List A (List B) List C Other	Responses were slow and deliberate. Did not attempt unknown words. _____ (Enter test name)	8	3
Writing Vocabulary	Able to write a few two and three letter high frequency words. Attempts show close visual similarity: $\frac{lik}{like}$ $\frac{kooL}{look}$		12	2
Hearing and Recording Sounds in Words	* A B C (D) E	Articulated slowly and made a good sound analysis of most words. Heard and recorded accurately some initial and final consonants.	23	3
Other tasks	Writing sample Story			

* Circle whatever was used

Useful strategic activity on text:

Problem strategic activity on text:

Useful strategic activity with words:

Problem strategic activity with words:

Useful strategic activity with letters:

Problem strategic activity with letters:

Summary statement:

Signature: _____

Useful strategic activity on text

Review the Running Records of book reading where the child is performing adequately (90 to 100 percent accuracy) and try to find some evidence of how effectively he works with the various kinds of information he can find in the print. Also look at the Concepts About Print items. Use these questions as a guide to your analysis of the records.

Location and movement

Does he control directional movement?
- — left to right?
- — top to bottom?
- — return sweep?

Does he locate particular information in print? What kind of information? Does he read word by word? If so, is this a new achievement (a plus because he is now trying to pull some things together) or an old habit cycling back (a minus showing that more recent learning is regressing under some strain, like text that is too hard for this reader at this time or not enough teacher assistance)?

Language

Does he control oral language well?

Does he read for meaning?

Does he control book language?

Does he have a good memory for text?

Does he read for the precise message?

Behaviour at difficulties

Does he seek help?

Does he try again?

Does he search for more information? How?
- — by rereading and taking another look?
- — by taking words apart, articulating letters or chunks?
- — by problem-solving by analogy?

Note unusual behaviours.

Substitutions

Do the error substitutions the child uses make sense with the previous text? (Meaning)

Do they continue an acceptable sentence in English? (Structure)

Could they occur in grammar for that sentence, up to that word?

Is the child getting to new words from known words by analogy? For example, from 'name' to 'game' or from 'play' and 'jump' to 'plump'.

Do some of the letters in the error match with letters in the text? (What use is the reader making of visual or graphic information?)

Self-correction

Does he return to the beginning of the line?

Does he reread from a few words back?

Does he repeat the word only?

Does he read on to the end of the line (a difficult and confusing behaviour for young readers)?

Does he repeat only the initial sound of a word?

Note unusual behaviour.

Cross-checking on information

Perhaps the child is at an early stage of text reading.

Does he ignore discrepancies?

Does he match his oral language with movement across text?

Does he check language structure with visual information?

Does he check the sounds he is saying with the printed letters?

Does he try to make language, movement and visual information line up together?

Useful strategic activity with words

Check Concepts About Print (C.A.P.), Text Reading, Writing Vocabulary, Hearing and Recording Sounds in Words, and Word Reading.

The visual features of words

On C.A.P. does he recognise line rearrangement?

On C.A.P. does he recognise word rearrangement?

On C.A.P. does he recognise that the first and last letters are rearranged?

On C.A.P. does he recognise that the medial letters are rearranged?

When reading text can he attend to detail?

Does he look for initial letters?

Does he notice final letters?

Does he recall some prior visual or writing experience of that word?

On writing tasks does the child know some words in every detail?

The sounds of words

Can the writer 'hear' the individual words in a sentence?

Can he articulate words slowly?

Can he break up words into sounds (as in writing a dictated sentence)?

Does he try to write new words using a sound analysis?

Does he build a consonant framework for a new word in writing?

Does he know that vowels are difficult and work at them?

Does he reread what he has written, carefully?

Useful strategic activity with letters

Check Concepts About Print (C.A.P.), Text Reading, Letter Identification, Writing Vocabulary, Hearing and Recording Sounds in Words, and Word Reading.

Movements used to make letters

Does the child form (write) some letters easily?

Does he form many letters without a copy?

Visual awareness

Which letters can he identify?

How does he identify them?

Which letters does he attend to when he is reading?

Could he detect an error because of a mismatch of letters?

(Which letters were difficult?)

(Which letters were confused one with another?)

Sounds

How does the child attempt a word in the Hearing and Recording Sounds in Words task?

Does he articulate hard words slowly?

Can he isolate the first sound of a word that he hears?

Can he give other words that start with the same sound?

Can he make/read/write other words that end with the same spelling pattern or inflection?

A completed summary sheet for an individual child

On Side 2 of the completed Summary Sheet (page 137) there is a useful example of how to bring together the results from the entire Observation Survey, using Chris's assessments as an example. (His full test records appear in the *An Observation Survey, The Video: Guidenotes*, Koefoed, Boocock and Wood, 1999). Chris's literacy achievement after one year in school was low.

Teachers being trained to administer the Observation Survey may find it useful to view how Chris responded to the observation tasks and discuss this summary in association with that viewing. Integrating the several pieces of information is not easy and requires practice and teaching experience but it is very useful for a teacher to try to complete a summary sheet like this. It also helps to discuss it with an interested colleague.

Using only the evidence which you have been reporting from the Observation Survey tasks, describe in a few lines the child's current way of responding. Point out what he can and cannot do on text reading. It may be that the child showed little evidence of processing on easy text, gave clear evidence of strengths and weaknesses on instructional texts, and showed signs of effective processing breaking down on hard texts. Characterise clearly the processing on the instructional level.

Indicate how the ways in which he works at the word and letter levels help or hinder his getting to the messages in reading and solving how to spell words in writing. This forces the teacher/observer to pull together all the relevant information, providing a state of the art overview. This could be the starting point of a programme of individual help.

The way of summarising the survey results adopted in the summary sheet for Chris looks comprehensive. However, it is incomplete in that it does not tell the teacher how to search for those strategic activities which relate one level of linguistic organisation to another; letters to words, and words to their meaningful contexts. We do not yet know much about changes in how the learner operates on several kinds of information at the same time, bringing different kinds of information together.

The way in which Chris' teacher wrote about his strategic activities on texts, words and letters in the summary that followed the Observation Survey is shown on page 137.

Chris' literacy achievement after one year in school was sufficiently low to warrant his referral to an early intervention. He gained access to supplementary individual instruction to help him catch up to his peers.

Useful strategic activity on text: Chris controls early reading behaviours. He appears to be gaining meaning from text, using his current control of language structures, words he knows and some visual information. At errors he uses information from both meaning and structure well and is just beginning to attend to some visual information. Some cross-checking on information is emerging.

Problem strategic activity on text: Chris mostly ignores errors and seems to be neglecting visual information. He waits for help and is unable to use any kind of information to attempt the more difficult words in text. Slow word reading, with just a few bursts of phrasing or intonation, probably limits his ability to hear language structures and group words together.

Useful strategic activity with words: He can recognise some known high-frequency words in reading. Occasionally he responds to the initial letters of unknown words in text. Chris knows how to write a few words in every detail and is very close to knowing some others. He can articulate words slowly, and knows how to hear and record a number of consonants and easy-to-hear vowels in simple words.

Problem strategic activity with words: Chris does not usually notice a mismatch between what he says and the visual information in the printed words. He is unable to use letter detail to assist him in solving novel words. In writing Chris controls a small core of words and produces these rather slowly. He is not always hearing or recording appropriate consonants or vowels in words.

Useful strategic activity with letters: While Chris sometimes seems to be led by an initial letter in his attempts, he is also using some visual information beyond the first letter. He is consistent in writing most letters reasonably clearly and usually puts letters in the correct order within words.

Problem strategic activity with letters: Chris is only just beginning to use letters as a kind of information to assist in solving words. When writing he reverses the odd letter and has a little difficulty with letter formation.

Summary statement: Chris is reading at a low level of beginning reading instruction. He is reading for meaning, drawing on his knowledge of language structure and his known reading vocabulary. At errors Chris is led by meaning and structure most of the time, and occasionally attends to some visual information. He is starting to cross-check on information. Chris's reading is slow and somewhat stilted with some intonation, but little expression and occasional phrasing. In writing, Chris knows how to write a limited number of high-frequency words with which he is secure. He is able to make quite a good sound analysis of short words recording dominant consonants and some vowels.

Signature: _____

A shorter summary for classroom teachers

The classroom teacher will have gathered much information about the child during the administration of the observation tasks. (She will have more understanding of these many observations if she has pulled together their collective message in the survey summary.) What does the Observation Survey now imply for her classroom practice? It is useful to ask the following questions.

With reading books

- What does the survey imply about the way new books are introduced to this child?

  — Is a rich introduction required?

  — Or is the child able to approach a new book with minimal preparation or guidance?

- Are there indications that other types of text need to be part of this child's reading?

- Do the books you are using support this child, allowing him to use what he knows in the service of trying new texts?

With writing

- Is there any aspect of writing that requires special attention?

- Does the child analyse the sounds in words and try to find ways of writing them?

- Does the child ask for feedback on his attempts?

- Does the child have a core vocabulary of high frequency words to support his story writing?

- What kinds of help does your classroom provide for the child to get to new words on his own?

Consistent patterns across children in reading and writing behaviours may provide evidence of emphases which were never intended or confusions not thought of.

- Do the results from several children tell you anything about:
  (a) the emphases of your programme?
  (b) the things you tend to be overlooking?

- Are there confusions to get rid of?

- Are there new things which you need to draw to children's attention?

- Do you have to think about more helpful and supportive texts?

- Do you need to provide more individual help for children to get their composed stories down on paper?

What are the next strategic activities to be emphasised?

- What changes in strategic activity would you wish to see these children making over the next three months of instruction?

- Will you expect them to be more independent of you? How is this to be achieved?

Summary for multiple assessments

At times it may be useful to record a history of assessments administered to a child, or groups of children, because they are receiving some supplementary help. An observation summary sheet for recording multiple testings is included on page 140. This may help teachers to think about trends in the changes occurring in the results of individual children, or for groups of children in the class or school.

OBSERVATION SUMMARY FOR MULTIPLE ASSESSMENTS

Name: _____

Date of Birth: _____

School: _____

SUMMARY OF RUNNING RECORD

Text Titles	$\dfrac{\text{Errors}}{\text{Running words}}$	Error Ratio	Accuracy Rate	Self-correction Ratio

Initial Assessment Date: _____

1. Easy _____ _____ 1: _____ _____ %: 1: _____

2. Instructional _____ _____ 1: _____ _____ %: 1: _____

3. Hard _____ _____ 1: _____ _____ %: 1: _____

Reassessment Date: _____

1. Easy _____ _____ 1: _____ _____ %: 1: _____

2. Instructional _____ _____ 1: _____ _____ %: 1: _____

3. Hard _____ _____ 1: _____ _____ %: 1: _____

Further Assessment Date: _____

1. Easy _____ _____ 1: _____ _____ %: 1: _____

2. Instructional _____ _____ 1: _____ _____ %: 1: _____

3. Hard _____ _____ 1: _____ _____ %: 1: _____

ASSESSMENT	L.I.		C.A.P.		Word Reading		Other Reading	Writing Vocabulary		Hearing Sounds in Words	
	54	Stanine	24	Stanine	15	Stanine	Test Score	No.	Stanine	37	Stanine
Initial assessment Date:											
Reassessment Date:											
Further Assessment (1)											
Further Assessment (2)											

RECOMMENDATIONS: (for class teacher, or for review, or further teaching, or further assessment)

11 The teacher and the observations

Sensitive observation: guiding literacy learning

An observant teacher must respond sensitively to the individual child's next step into new territory. How can she do this?

- She must be familiar with what the child already knows.

- She must be close at hand as he reads and writes.

- She must know how to support his next leap forward.

- She must allow enough space for the child to become an independent learner.

Such knowledge allows the teacher to guide the literacy learning of individual children. The same information allows a teacher to monitor the progress of groups of young children. She can quickly find out when children need a change of pace or a change of direction in order to maximise their opportunities to learn. A teaching programme can be organised so that:

- the teacher can observe how children are working and learning

- the teacher can make and keep records

- the teacher can monitor the progress of the competent children at spaced intervals

- the teacher can monitor and guide the teaching of the less competent children at frequent intervals.

The value of observing reading behaviours

Running Records of text reading can be used whenever oral reading is appropriate. Teachers can use them in many ways.

1   **Capturing behaviour for later consideration.** When teachers take a Running Record as the child reads his book they find they notice more about what the child is trying to do. They can also look back over this record, replay in their minds exactly what the child said and did, check on the validity of their assumptions, and think about the behaviour. The record captures the behaviour of the moment.

2   **Quantifying the record.** If a teacher counts how many words there are in the text which the child reads she can quickly turn this behaviour into an accuracy score, and relate this to a gradient of book difficulty (see page 68). Her statement might read 'Unaided he reads Book Level 7 with 95% accuracy but Book Level 8 with 87% accuracy.'

3   **A cumulative record.** Change over time can be captured with such records taken from time to time, during the child's usual reading to the teacher.

4   **Placement.** From such records teachers can place children in groups or classes in a school. A child who is changing his school can be quickly checked to see at what level he will succeed in a new school.

5   **For critical decisions.** Critical decisions about giving the young child special assistance of some kind, or rapid promotion, or a referral to the school psychologist can be supported with a report on the child's reading behaviour on texts, from Running Records. I advised my child psychology students to ask for such records (partly because it puts a responsibility on teachers to be observant and partly because it saves the psychologist's time).

6   **To establish text difficulty.** I think of reading progress as being able to read increasingly difficult texts with accuracy and understanding. Running Records are used by teachers to try out a child on a book to test the difficulty level of the text in relation to the child's competencies. Having such a behavioural record of exactly how a pupil reads a particular text gives teachers confidence to allow different children to move through different books at different speeds. They know they can still keep track of individual progress.

7   **Observing particular difficulties.** Running Records provide opportunities for observing children's confusions and difficulties. The teacher records every correct response with a tick (check) and records all error and self-correction behaviour. This provides evidence of how the child works on words in text, what success he has, and what strengths he brings to the task. A teacher can quickly decide what might be the next most profitable learning point for that child and can test this out during teaching.

8   **For research purposes.** The records of well-trained teachers taken on a series of texts with a known gradient of difficulty can yield a ranking of students on book level by accuracy. These will correlate highly with test scores in the first two or three years of schooling.

The value of observing writing behaviours

Standard ways of observing early writing behaviours supplement the teacher's daily observation in the classroom. They provide evidence of where the child's resources for text writing may be limited and need some special attention — knowledge of letters, sounds, taking words apart and constructing words — and the size of the pool of knowledge that makes up the child's writing vocabulary.

The teacher may become aware of discrepancies between reading and writing progress, with strength in one not supporting the other. Seeing these two literacy activities out of balance the teacher will take opportunities to reinforce one with the other, calling the child's attention to the ways in which reading can help with writing and vice versa.

Teachers will also find out which children need more time and assistance as they work on independent writing tasks. It may be a question of showing some children again how to use classroom resources, or of delegating a peer to become a helper, or using some of a classroom assistant's time and, for the hardest to teach, the help will need to be given by the teacher herself.

Information for the education system

There are several ways that an education system, a school system or a cluster of classes in a school can gain information on performance in that system by observing reading and writing behaviours.

1   **Programme emphases.** If a supervising teacher takes records of text reading with a wide sample of children she will quickly discover if the teaching programme is out of balance. Word-by-word reading, spelling out words, not attending to meaning, ignoring letter cues or word endings — all these will stand out clearly in the records and so will the good outcomes, like the child getting it all together smoothly, working on words in ways which surprise the teacher, enjoying the stories and commenting on possible plot and character outcomes, relating what is being read to other experiences.

2   **New programme features.** If a programme is changed and new emphases are introduced, Running Records can be used to monitor the effects. Do the desired changes in children's processing of texts show up on the records? Can you see any adverse effects of the new teaching? Do the records suggest any minor adjustments now, without waiting for the summative assessment at the end of the year?

3   **Training teachers.** A Running Record is an assessment which leads the teacher to ask herself questions about the child's needs. As she takes a record a teacher may discover new behaviours and begin to think about learning in new ways. For example, sometimes the reader goes back, repeating himself, rerunning the correct message. Why does he do that? He was correct. Could it be that the child is surprised by what he read and has rerun to monitor his own behaviour to ensure that it is correct? Monitoring one's own language activities has a great deal of relevance for learning. It is important and needs to be encouraged.

Another contribution to teacher training occurs when teachers keep today's record as a baseline, and over several occasions observe the child again, capturing progress. It is informative to look back at the records of the changes that have occurred.

4   **Information for lay persons.** Two groups who make demands on teachers in New Zealand are parents and administrators. We have been surprised at how impressed both groups have been with two outcomes of Running Records taken over time. Teachers have used graphs of the reading progress (see page 77) of children through their reading books in their appeals for resources to school management committees and school boards. Parents have also been reassured by such records and by sharing with the teacher the folios of work which show the child's progressions in writing or the change over time in Writing Vocabulary. We have found that behavioural records, if thoughtfully planned, communicate clearly to lay persons interested in education. Note that it is not the actual Running Records that have been shared with lay people.

In addition to the Running Records the other observation procedures (Concepts About Print, Writing Vocabulary, Hearing and Recording Sounds in Words, and Letter Identification) reported in this early intervention survey can show teachers which children do not understand some basic concepts about books and print, or who is trying to read with little knowledge of letters, or which children seem to know words but are not noticing letter sequences within them. *The confusions of young readers belong to all beginners: it is just that the successful children sort themselves out and the unsuccessful do not.* It is helpful to sort out confusions before they consolidate into unwanted habits.

To minimise carelessness, bias and variability in observation records:

- there has to be a gradient of difficulty in the texts selected by teachers for children to read

- and the teachers must be well trained. Six teachers scoring the same record should all get the same results. One teacher reading another teacher's record should be able to replay what the child actually said.

Information to support an early intervention for some children

Early identification of children at risk in literacy learning has proved to be possible and should be systematically carried out not later than one year after a child has entered a formal programme. This gives the shy and slow children time to settle in and adjust to the demands of a teacher. It also overcomes the problems of trying to identify those who fail to learn to read before some of them have had a chance to learn what reading and writing are about. In many ways it is sensible to try to predict this only after all children have had some equivalent opportunities to respond to good teaching.

At the beginning of formal literacy instruction children will differ:

- in their awareness of the detail in print

- in what they find confusing about print

- and in the ways they choose to work with print.

What is salient differs from child to child. Children can respond to an intervention especially tailored to their needs in individual instruction, but classroom teachers who find these observation tasks useful for identifying children who need extra help must still consider how they should teach such children. For the lowest 20 percent of the age group classroom attention alone is not likely to solve the problem.

Most of the assumptions about reading achievement and reading difficulty would not lead us to expect that children who have difficulty would ever catch up to their classmates, or make continued normal progress. They would have to learn at greatly accelerated rates of progress to do that.

The Reading Recovery development project questioned whether such assumptions were well founded. We asked, 'How many children given a quality intervention early in their schooling could achieve and maintain normal levels of progress?' In other words, for what percentage of the children having reading difficulties was it really a question of never having got started with appropriate learning patterns?

A quality model of Reading Recovery (see Clay, 2005a and b) provides several dimensions of assistance for a child in addition to his class programme.

- First, a shift to one-to-one instruction allows the teacher to design a series of lessons that begin where the child is, and not where the curriculum is. Any grouping of children for teaching forces a compromise on this position.

- Then, daily instruction increases the power of the intervention.

- The teacher strives to make the child independent of her (to overcome one of the major problems of remedial tuition) and she never does for the child anything that she can teach him to do for himself.

- Acceleration is achieved by all the above means and also because the teacher never wastes valuable learning time on teaching something the child does not need to learn. She moves him to a harder text as soon as this is feasible but backs such progressions with quantities of easy reading.

- From sound theory of the reading process the child is taught 'how to …'. How to carry out operations to solve problems in text, how to monitor his reading, how to check his options, how to work independently on print.

It is not enough to have systematic observation procedures which monitor the progress of individual children. To be really effective a powerful second chance intervention must be provided. It should be viable within the education system and have its own checks and balances to give quality assurance and quality control. It needs to 'live in' and adapt to small and large schools, small and large education systems, and different populations and literacy programmes.

Many interventions for children with special needs never get to consider the following issues. It is necessary to demonstrate:

- that the intervention can work with children

- that teachers can be trained to make it work

- that the intervention can fit into the organisation of the school

- that it can be run and maintained within an education system.

In considering those issues I have learned that quality control of an intervention to recover children having difficulty requires teachers who can make sensitive observations in systematic ways, but this is not sufficient. To make an early intervention viable across time it is necessary:

- that teachers be trained concurrently in the conceptual and practical aspects of the intervention

- that they understand the teaching procedures

- that they apply them consistently and critically

- that they can articulate and discuss their assumptions

- that they are supervised for a probationary period

- that those training teachers thoroughly understand the theory on which the intervention and procedures were based

- that the teacher is a member of a school team which is mounting the intervention to reduce reading and writing difficulties in that school

- that professional development of teachers continues so that changes to the intervention arising from new research can be quickly translated into ways of retraining and modifying the practice of teachers

- that the education system supplies resources for early intervention to save a higher outlay later to provide for older children still struggling with literacy.

An overview

Low achievers cannot profit from group instruction as easily as well-prepared children in the early years of school, so we need to fine-tune our instruction adjusting to their individual learning histories rather than buy another new curriculum or switch to a new method.

Systematic observation allows teachers to go to where the child is and begin teaching from there. Some teachers say, 'When you reach the point where our programme starts you will be "ready" for instruction; until then you are not ready.' It makes more sense for the teacher to become a sensitive observer of children in order to help them make the transitions that have been planned for them.

A year at school will give most children a chance to settle, and to begin to try their abilities in literacy. Systematic observation will uncover which children are forming good ways of working on print, habits, skills, whatever you want to conceptualise as central to learning at this stage. It makes good psychological and administrative sense to find out before too long which children are becoming confused by standard educational practices, so that they can be offered alternative approaches to the same goals.

The teacher must monitor the changes that are occurring in the individual learner if she is going to fine-tune her lesson series. Otherwise she will be holding back the fast movers or dragging along the slow movers, already out of their depth. Low achievers can learn quite well if the teacher uses individual assessments to guide her teaching interactions with a particular child. The teacher needs assessments that tell her about the child's existing repertoire and how he is getting to those responses, and whether he is relating information from one area of competency to another. In literacy learning we are looking at ways of capturing:

- process

- repertoire

- strategic activity

- problem-solving (see Clay, 2001).

We want to record change over time in all these things as the child moves up a gradient of difficulty with increasing independence of teacher support.

If instruction is flexible enough to respect individuality in the first stages of new learning it can bring children gradually to the point where group instruction can proceed effectively with few confusions.

Observational instruments can arise from theory and can lead to research. A variety of theories may lead to observational tasks: measurement theory, or the psychology of learning, or developmental theory about change over time, or the study of individual differences, or theories of social factors and the influences of contexts on learning. The observational tasks in this survey direct teacher attention to the ways in which children are finding sources of information in texts and working with that information.

Typically this approach calls for time with individuals. There is an enormous mental barrier which says, 'This is not a teacher's role.' I say, emphatically, it is! If the teacher can be more effective because she seeks and uses observational data to inform her teaching then we need tasks which fit easily into the busy schedule of a teacher's day. If possible we must find good observational appraisals which have sound measurement characteristics and that can be used by the teacher on the run in day-to-day classroom practice. Such assessments can be compared from one time to the next, from one classroom to the next, and from one school to the next.

Stanine tables

Stanine scores for tasks: New Zealand

Stanines for 5.00 – 5.50 years (for 223 children in 2000)

Letter Identification
(N = 223; Score Range: 0–54; Mean = 39.0; SE = 1.05; SD = 15.7)

Test Score	0–3	4–12	13–27	28–42	43–49	50–52	53	— 54 —	
Stanine Grp	1	2	3	4	5	6	7	8	9

Concepts About Print
(N = 223; Score Range: 0–24; Mean = 13.5; SE = 0.23; SD = 3.5)

Test Score	0–7	8–9	10–11	12–13	14	15–16	17–18	19	20+
Stanine Grp	1	2	3	4	5	6	7	8	9

Clay Word Reading
(N = 223; Score Range: 0–15; Mean = 4.3; SE = 0.30; SD = 4.5)

Test Score	— 0 —		1	2	3–4	5–8	9–11	12–14	15
Stanine Grp	1	2	3	4	5	6	7	8	9

Writing Vocabulary
(N = 223; Score Range: 0–130; Mean = 12.9; SE = 0.89; SD = 13.4)

Test Score	0	1	2–3	4–6	7–11	12–18	19–32	33–48	49+
Stanine Grp	1	2	3	4	5	6	7	8	9

Hearing and Recording Sounds in Words
(N = 223; Score Range: 0–37; Mean = 15.6; SE = 0.77; SD = 11.6)

Test Score	0	1	2–4	5–11	12–18	19–26	27–33	34–36	37
Stanine Grp	1	2	3	4	5	6	7	8	9

Duncan Word Reading
(N = 223; Score Range: 0–23; Mean = 7.4; SE = 0.48; SD = 7.2)

Test Score	— 0 —		1	2–3	4–7	8–13	14–19	20–22	23
Stanine Grp	1	2	3	4	5	6	7	8	9

NEW ZEALAND

Stanines for 5.51 – 6.00 years (for 170 children in 2000)

Letter Identification
(N = 170; Score Range: 0–54; Mean = 46.6; SE = 0.93; SD = 12.1)

Test Score	0–10	11–35	36–46	47–51	52	53	— — — 54 — — —		
Stanine Grp	1	2	3	4	5	6	7	8	9

Concepts About Print
(N = 170; Score Range: 0–24, Mean = 15.5; SE = 0.28; SD = 3.7)

Test Score	0–8	9–11	12–13	14–15	16–17	18	19–20	21–22	23–24
Stanine Grp	1	2	3	4	5	6	7	8	9

Clay Word Reading
(N = 170; Score Range: 0–15; Mean = 7.7; SE = 0.39; SD = 5.11)

Test Score	0	1	2–3	4–6	7–10	11–13	14	— 15 —	
Stanine Grp	1	2	3	4	5	6	7	8	9

Writing Vocabulary
(N = 170; Score Range: 0–130; Mean = 23.8; SE = 1.33; SD = 17.4)

Test Score	0–2	3–5	6–8	9–15	16–26	27–37	38–48	49–58	59+
Stanine Grp	1	2	3	4	5	6	7	8	9

Hearing and Recording Sounds in Words
(N = 170; Score Range: 0–37; Mean = 23.6; SE = 0.81; SD = 10.5)

Test Score	0–1	2–7	8–15	16–22	23–29	30–33	34–36	— 37 —	
Stanine Grp	1	2	3	4	5	6	7	8	9

Duncan Word Reading
(N = 170; Score Range: 0–23; Mean = 13.1; SE = 0.57; SD = 7.4)

Test Score	1	2	3–6	7–11	12–16	17–20	21–22	— 23 —	
Stanine Grp	1	2	3	4	5	6	7	8	9

NEW ZEALAND

Stanines for 6.01 – 6.50 years (for 230 children in 2000)

Letter Identification
(N = 230; Score Range: 0–54; Mean = 50.7; SE = 0.50; SD = 7.5)

Test Score	0–34	35–48	49–50	51	52	53	––– 54 –––		
Stanine Grp	1	2	3	4	5	6	7	8	9

Concepts About Print
(N = 230; Score Range: 0–24, Mean = 18.0; SE = 0.23; SD = 3.4)

Test Score	0–11	12–14	15–16	17	18–19	20	21–22	23	24
Stanine Grp	1	2	3	4	5	6	7	8	9

Clay Word Reading
(N = 230; Score Range: 0–15; Mean = 11.4; SE = 0.28; SD = 4.3)

Test Score	0–1	2–4	5–9	10–12	13–14	–––– 15 ––––			
Stanine Grp	1	2	3	4	5	6	7	8	9

Writing Vocabulary
(N = 230; Score Range: 0–130; Mean = 42.7; SE = 1.51; SD = 22.9)

Test Score	0–4	5–13	14–25	26–36	37–49	50–59	60–69	70–83	84+
Stanine Grp	1	2	3	4	5	6	7	8	9

Hearing and Recording Sounds in Words
(N = 230; Score Range: 0–37; Mean = 30.7; SE = 0.56; SD = 8.4)

Test Score	0–8	9–19	20–27	28–32	33–35	36	–– 37 ––		
Stanine Grp	1	2	3	4	5	6	7	8	9

Duncan Word Reading
(N = 230; Score Range: 0–23; Mean = 18.5; SE = 0.39; SD = 5.9)

Test Score	0–3	4–10	11–16	17–20	21–22	–––– 23 ––––			
Stanine Grp	1	2	3	4	5	6	7	8	9

NEW ZEALAND

Stanines for 6.51 – 7.00 years (for 173 children in 2000)

Letter Identification
(N = 173; Score Range: 0–54; Mean = 51.6; SE = 0.49; SD = 6.4)

Test Score	0–40	41–50	51–52	53		– – – 54 – – –			
Stanine Grp	1	2	3	4	5	6	7	8	9

Concepts About Print
(N = 173; Score Range: 0–24, Mean = 18.7; SE = 0.24; SD = 3.2)

Test Score	0–13	14–15	16–17	18	19–20	21	22–23	– 24 –	
Stanine Grp	1	2	3	4	5	6	7	8	9

Clay Word Reading
(N = 173; Score Range: 0–15; Mean = 13.0; SE = 0.24; SD = 3.1)

Test Score	0–4	5–10	11–12	13	14	– – – – 15 – – – –			
Stanine Grp	1	2	3	4	5	6	7	8	9

Writing Vocabulary
(N = 173; Score Range: 0–130; Mean = 51.0; SE = 1.69; SD = 22.3)

Test Score	0–8	9–25	26–35	36–45	46–56	57–66	67–80	81–99	100+
Stanine Grp	1	2	3	4	5	6	7	8	9

Hearing and Recording Sounds in Words
(N = 173; Score Range: 0–37; Mean = 33.2; SE = 0.49; SD = 6.5)

Test Score	0–14	15–28	29–32	33–35	36	– – 37 – –			
Stanine Grp	1	2	3	4	5	6	7	8	9

Duncan Word Reading
(N = 173; Score Range: 0–23; Mean = 20.4; SE = 0.36; SD = 4.7)

Test Score	0–3	4–10	11–16	17–20	21–22	– – – – 23 – – – –			
Stanine Grp	1	2	3	4	5	6	7	8	9

Stanine scores for tasks: Canada

Use the fall stanines from August–November, mid-year stanines from December–February, and end of year from March–June.

Letter Identification									
Stanine	1	2	3	4	5	6	7	8	9
Fall	0–23	24–36	37–45	46–49	50–51	52	53	54	–
Mid-Year	0–47	48–50	51–52	53	54	–	–	–	–
Year-End	0–50	51–52	53	54	–	–	–	–	–

Word Reading									
Stanine	1	2	3	4	5	6	7	8	9
Fall	0	1		2–3	4–6	7–10	11–13	14	15
Mid-Year	0–3	4–7	8–10	11–12	13	14–15	–	–	–
Year-End	0–9	10–11	12–13	14	15	–	–	–	–

Concepts About Print									
Stanine	1	2	3	4	5	6	7	8	9
Fall	0–3	4–8	9–11	12–13	14–15	16–17	18	19–20	21–24
Mid-Year	0–12	13–14	15–16	17–18	19	20–21	22	23	24
Year-End	0–15	16–18	19	20	21	22	23	24	–

Writing Vocabulary									
Stanine	1	2	3	4	5	6	7	8	9
Fall	0–1	2	3–5	6–8	9–13	14–20	21–28	29–38	39+
Mid-Year	0–10	11–15	16–23	24–29	30–38	39–47	48–55	56–66	67+
Year-End	0–17	18–27	28–36	37–43	44–51	52–58	59–68	69–82	83+

Hearing and Recording Sounds in Words									
Stanine	1	2	3	4	5	6	7	8	9
Fall	0–2	3–6	7–12	13–19	20–27	28–31	32–34	35–36	37
Mid-Year	0–20	21–26	27–31	32–34	35	36	37	–	–
Year-End	0–27	28–32	33–34	35	36	37	–	–	–

Stanine scores for tasks: United Kingdom (England and Wales)

Stanine scores for 5.00 – 5.50 years (for 254 children in 2009)

Letter Identification (LI)

Scoring: *N* = 254; *Mean* = 45.01; *SD* = 9.28; *Range* = 0-54.

Stanine Group	1	2	3	4	5	6	7	8	9
Test Score	0–23	24–30	31–41	42–46	47–49	50	51–52	–	53–54

Concepts About Print (CAP)

Scoring: *N* = 254; *Mean* = 12.35; *SD* = 3.74; *Range* = 0-24.

Stanine Group	1	2	3	4	5	6	7	8	9
Test Score	0–5	6–7	8	9–11	12	13–14	15–16	17	18–24

Duncan Word Test (DWT)

Scoring: *N* = 254; *Mean* = 9.93; *SD* = 6.58; *Range* = 0-23.

Stanine Group	1	2	3	4	5	6	7	8	9
Test Score	–	0–1	2–3	4–7	8–11	12–14	15–19	20–21	22–23

Writing Vocabulary (WV)

Scoring: *N* = 250; *Mean* = 12.68; *SD* = 10.08; *Range* = 0-MAX.

Stanine Group	1	2	3	4	5	6	7	8	9
Test Score	–	0–1	2–3	4–7	8–12	13–18	19–24	25–30	31+

Hearing and Recording Sounds in Words (HRSIW)

Scoring: *N* = 250; *Mean* = 22.28; *SD* = 10.77; *Range* = 0-37.

Stanine Group	1	2	3	4	5	6	7	8	9
Test Score	0–1	2–5	6–11	12–20	21–27	28–31	32–34	35	36–37

UNITED KINGDOM

Stanine scores for 5.51 – 6.00 years (for 251 children in 2009)

Letter Identification (LI)

Scoring: *N* = 251; *Mean* = 48.47; *SD* = 8.15; *Range* = 0-54.

Stanine Group	1	2	3	4	5	6	7	8	9
Test Score	0–24	25–41	42–46	47–49	50–51	52	53	54	54

Concepts About Print (CAP)

Scoring: *N* = 251; *Mean* = 15.00; *SD* = 4.31; *Range* = 0-24.

Stanine Group	1	2	3	4	5	6	7	8	9
Test Score	0–6	7–8	9–11	12–13	14–16	17	18–19	20	21–24

Duncan Word Test (DWT)

Scoring: *N* = 249; *Mean* = 15.41; *SD* = 7.37; *Range* = 0-23.

Stanine Group	1	2	3	4	5	6	7	8	9
Test Score	–	0–3	4–8	9–14	15–19	20–21	22	23	23

Writing Vocabulary (WV)

Scoring: *N* = 249; *Mean* = 22.22; *SD* = 14.70; *Range* = 0-MAX.

Stanine Group	1	2	3	4	5	6	7	8	9
Test Score	–	0–4	5–9	10–16	17–23	24–32	33–39	40–51	52+

Hearing and Recording Sounds in Words (HRSIW)

Scoring: *N* = 248; *Mean* = 28.14; *SD* = 9.94; *Range* = 0-37.

Stanine Group	1	2	3	4	5	6	7	8	9
Test Score	0–2	3–10	11–22	23–29	30–33	34–35	36	37	37

UNITED KINGDOM

Stanine scores for 6.01 – 6.50 years (for 248 children in 2009)

Letter Identification (LI)

Scoring: N = 248; Mean = 51.26; SD = 3.63; Range = 0-54.

Stanine Group	1	2	3	4	5	6	7	8	9
Test Score	0–44	45–47	48–49	50–51	52	–	53	54	54

Concepts About Print (CAP)

Scoring: N = 249; Mean = 17.48; SD = 3.56; Range = 0-24.

Stanine Group	1	2	3	4	5	6	7	8	9
Test Score	0–9	10–12	13–14	15–16	17	18–20	21	22	23–24

Duncan Word Test (DWT)

Scoring: N = 247; Mean = 19.58; SD = 4.70; Range = 0-23.

Stanine Group	1	2	3	4	5	6	7	8	9
Test Score	0–8	9–12	13–16	17–20	21	22	23	23	23

Writing Vocabulary (WV)

Scoring: N = 244; Mean = 29.97; SD = 15.06; Range = 0-MAX.

Stanine Group	1	2	3	4	5	6	7	8	9
Test Score	0–8	9–13	14–18	19–23	24–31	32–39	40–48	49–59	60+

Hearing and Recording Sounds in Words (HRSIW)

Scoring: N = 244; Mean = 33.95; SD = 4.11; Range = 0-37.

Stanine Group	1	2	3	4	5	6	7	8	9
Test Score	0–23	24–28	29–31	32–34	35	36	37	37	37

Stanine scores for 6.51 – 7.00 years (for 224 children in 2009)

Letter Identification (LI)

Scoring: *N* = 224; *Mean* = 51.85; *SD* = 3.31; *Range* = 0-54.

Stanine Group	1	2	3	4	5	6	7	8	9
Test Score	0–44	45–48	49–50	51–52	–	53	54	54	54

Concepts About Print (CAP)

Scoring: *N* = 224; *Mean* = 18.92; *SD* = 3.39; *Range* = 0-24.

Stanine Group	1	2	3	4	5	6	7	8	9
Test Score	0–11	12–14	15–16	17	18–19	20–21	22	23	24

Duncan Word Test (DWT)

Scoring: *N* = 224; *Mean* = 20.80; *SD* = 4.18; *Range* = 0-23.

Stanine Group	1	2	3	4	5	6	7	8	9
Test Score	0–8	9–15	16–19	20–21	22	23	23	23	23

Writing Vocabulary (WV)

Scoring: *N* = 224; *Mean* = 36.56; *SD* = 16.59; *Range* = 0-MAX.

Stanine Group	1	2	3	4	5	6	7	8	9
Test Score	0–8	9–16	17–22	23–29	30–39	40–48	49–58	59–67	68+

Hearing and Recording Sounds in Words (HRSIW)

Scoring: *N* = 223; *Mean* = 34.49; *SD* = 5.18; *Range* = 0-37.

Stanine Group	1	2	3	4	5	6	7	8	9
Test Score	0–21	22–30	31–33	34–35	36	37	37	37	37

Stanine scores for tasks: United States

Use fall stanines August–November, mid-year stanines December–February, and year-end stanines March–July.

Letter Identification									
Stanine	1	2	3	4	5	6	7	8	9
Fall	0–43	44–47	48–49	50–51	52	–	53	–	54
Mid-Year	0–50	51	52	–	53	–	–	–	54
Year-End	0–51	52	–	53	–	–	–	–	54

Concepts About Print									
Stanine	1	2	3	4	5	6	7	8	9
Fall	0–7	8–10	11–12	13–14	15	16–17	18	19–20	21
Mid-Year	0–12	13–14	15–16	17	18–19	20	21	22	23
Year-End	0–15	16–17	18	19–20	21	22	–	23	24

Ohio Word Test									
Stanine	1	2	3	4	5	6	7	8	9
Fall	0	1	2–3	4–5	6–9	10–14	15–18	19	20
Mid-Year	0–6	7–9	10–12	13–15	16–18	19	–	–	20
Year-End	0–14	15–16	17–18	19	–	–	–	–	20

Writing Vocabulary									
Stanine	1	2	3	4	5	6	7	8	9
Fall	0–3	4–6	7–9	10–14	15–20	21–27	28–34	35–44	45+
Mid-Year	0–16	17–24	25–30	31–37	38–45	46–52	53–61	62–72	73+
Year-End	0–26	27–35	36–43	44–51	52–59	60–68	69–78	79–91	92+

Hearing and Recording Sounds in Words									
Stanine	1	2	3	4	5	6	7	8	9
Fall	0–8	9–15	16–22	23–27	28–31	32–34	35	36	37
Mid-Year	0–26	27–30	31–33	34	35	36	–	–	37
Year-End	0–31	32–33	34	35	36	–	–	–	37

Text Reading Level									
Stanine	1	2	3	4	5	6	7	8	9
Fall	0*[1]	0*[2]	1	2	3	4–5	6–12	14–20	22
Mid-Year	0–2	3–4	5–6	7–9	10–12	14–16	18–22	24–28	30
Year-End	0–6	7–10	12–14	16	18–22	24	26–28	–	30

*The raw scores in this stanine do not correspond to the mean and standard deviation for this task. They have been adjusted for the purpose of student selection.

[1] A child who **does not** read the Level 1 text with 90% accuracy *even after it has first been read entirely by the teacher* is assigned a score of zero for data collection. A child who has an opportunity to read his own dictated text as written and reread by the teacher is also assigned a score of zero. Use stanine 1 for student selection in fall.

[2] A child who **does** read the Level 1 text with 90% accuracy *only after it has first been read entirely by the teacher* is assigned a score of zero for data collection. Use stanine 2 for student selection in the fall.

Appendices

Appendix 1

Historical notes on the Observation Survey

Early development

The Observation Survey developed over the period 1963–78 and has subsequently been revised. The research began with Marie Clay's doctoral dissertation entitled *Emergent Reading Behaviour* presented to the University of Auckland in 1966 and examined by professors Ralph Winterbourn, University of Auckland, Arthur Fieldhouse, Victoria University of Wellington, and Helen Robinson, University of Chicago. The findings were reported at the Second World Congress of the International Reading Association in Copenhagen in 1968 under the sponsorship of professors Helen Robinson and Albert J. Harris.

Resulting research and publications appeared in peer-reviewed educational and psychological journals over the next decade (Clay, 1967, 1968, 1969, 1970a, 1971 with Imlach, 1974a and b, 1975a). The original study of English-speaking children was replicated with four groups differing according to the language spoken in their homes (Advantaged in English, Average English, two Maori parents, and two Samoan parents, reported in 1970b, 1971, 1975b and 1976).

All the observation procedures for reading were published in the first edition of *The Early Detection of Reading Difficulties: A Diagnostic Survey* in 1972b (Letter Identification, Word Reading, Running Records and Concepts About Print). Writing Vocabulary and Hearing and Recording Sounds in Words were added following research and development trials between 1973 and 1978 and appeared in the second edition. A developing theoretical analysis has been recorded in books and articles published across three decades (Clay, 1972a, 1979a, 1985, 1991, 1998, 2001).

Publication history

The first edition of *The Early Detection of Reading Difficulties: A Diagnostic Survey* (Clay, 1972b) was published in Auckland by Heinemann Educational Books. In the same year some theory for teachers about early literacy acquisition derived directly from the earlier dissertation and the replication study was published in *Reading: The Patterning of Complex Behaviour*.

Second editions of both books were published in 1979 following the development of the Reading Recovery intervention. Research results from the early years of that development were included in those editions.

A third edition of the assessment survey was published in 1985 with extensive revisions as more information was obtained from use of the observation instruments in the field, from the results of early intervention research, from a predictive validity study and from more theoretical discussions about change over time in literacy competencies available in the literature.

A major revision of *Reading: The Patterning of Complex Behaviour* resulted in a change of title to *Becoming Literate: The Construction of Inner Control* (Clay, 1991) (which was in an historical sense a third edition). It was followed in 1993 by *An Observation Survey of Early Literacy Achievement*, a title more in keeping with the purposes and applications for which the material was used, reflecting also some further shifts in academic analyses.

Historically, the theory moved ahead of the Observation Survey and in 2001 *Change Over Time in Children's Literacy Development* was published. In 2002, the second edition of *An Observation Survey of Early Literacy Achievement* was completed.

There are four alternative test booklets for the Concepts About Print assessment: they are called *Sand* (1972c), *Stones* (1979b), *Follow Me, Moon* (2000c) and *No Shoes* (2000d). Stand-alone books *Running Records for Classroom Teachers* and *Concepts About Print* were published in 2000a and b.

A bilingual Spanish-English version of *An Observation Survey of Early Literacy Achievement* was authored by Escamilla, Andrade, Basurto and Ruiz and published by Heinemann in USA (1996) and a Maori-English reconstruction was compiled by C. Rau and published by Kia Ata Mai Educational Trust in Ngaruawahia in 1998. A Gaelic edition of *An Observation Survey of Early Literacy Achievement* was published in 2006. For each of those developments at least two Concepts About Print test booklets are available.

Independent testimony

Three references to peer-reviewed publications are provided to illustrate that *An Observation Survey of Early Literacy Achievement* was subjected to careful scrutiny by researchers.

The following quote is from Jane Hurry's article entitled 'What is so special about Reading Recovery?' published in *The Curriculum Journal* (1996, page 97) in the United Kingdom.

> This test battery includes letter identification, concepts about print, a word test, writing vocabulary, dictation and a test of reading based on 'real books' graded by difficulty. In the United Kingdom evaluation of Reading Recovery this was found to be the most sensitive of the measures used to assess children's reading ability at this age (including the British Ability Scale of Word Reading and the Neale Analysis of Reading) reported in Sylva and Hurry (1995). Elements of this assessment pack have been used in many Local Education Authorities for some time to identify children at Key Stage 1 with special needs. This is not surprising as it compares favourably with other diagnostic batteries suitable for use with this group of children in a school setting.

In 1999 *The International Journal of Educational Research* devoted a whole issue to a study entitled 'Investigating the relationship between students' *attentive-inattentive* behaviours in the classroom and their literacy progress', by K.J. Rowe and K.S. Rowe. The authors reported on the literacy achievement of their sample on two testing occasions using three sub-tests from the *Woodcock Language Proficiency Battery* (1993) and all six of the measures comprising *An Observation Survey of Early Literacy Achievement* (Clay, 1993b) and the *Record of Oral Language* (Clay et al., 1983).

In March 2012, following a rigorous, two-stage review process, *An Observation Survey of Early Literacy Achievement* received the highest possible ratings on five technical standards from the National Center for the Response to Intervention (NCRTI). The NCRTI was established by the American Institutes for Research, Vanderbilt University, and the University of Kansas through the US Department of Education's Office of Special Education and was 'charged with providing technical assistance to states and districts to implement proven response to intervention (RTI) methods' (D'Agostino, 2012). The NCRTI's ratings and descriptions of assessment tools are intended to inform and assist educators as they select screening tools that are valid, reliable, and evidence-based.

To prepare for the technical review, D'Agostino (2012) applied a one-parameter item response theory (IRT) measurement model to create an Observation Survey total score, or one common literacy scale. Subsequent analyses revealed evidence meeting NCRTI's criteria at the highest levels and confirmed:

1) classification accuracy in that the fall Observation Survey total score has a .87 receiver operator characteristic value in predicting spring performance on an external measure, the Slosson Oral Reading Test – Revised;

2) generalisability with evidence from multiple years of random sample data;

3) reliability with an alpha coefficient of .87 and a split-half coefficient of .89 for the 2009–2010 random sample total scores for 7,926 students;

4) validity, demonstrated by correlations greater than .70 with a range of reading measures; and

5) disaggregated reliability, validity, and classification accuracy for sub-groups of children revealed by analysing random sample data for African American and Hispanic students.

Resultantly, the NCRTI (2012) confirmed that the Observation Survey is an appropriate, evidence-based tool for identifying children at risk of literacy failure.

Appendix 2

Validity and reliability reports for the Observation Survey tasks

Content validity: The tasks of the Observation Survey were derived from common literacy behaviors of children as observed by Clay (1982). These tasks have been shown to be sensitive indicators of behaviors that support reading and writing acquisition. Each of the six tasks assesses an area of literacy knowledge which provides an essential foundation for progress in reading and writing. The content of the tasks represents what is actually taught in the classroom, and is aligned with many literacy standards at grade level.

Construct validity: The interrelationships among the task scores and correlations between task scores and external measures have been examined to document construct validity. Correlations of scores at 6:0 years for the 100 New Zealand children in the original study with test and behaviour variables were presented in the original dissertation (Clay, 1966). The correlation between Word Reading and Concepts About Print was .79, and the value between Word Reading and Letter Identification was .85. Robinson (1973) reported a .82 correlation between Word Reading and Writing Vocabulary.

Using only school entrants the New Zealand Ministry of Education correlated four subscores with the total score on Concepts About Print. The correlations of part with whole score were high for knowing how reading is carried out ($r = .93$), punctuation ($r = .68$), concepts about print ($r = .84$), but attention to sequences of letters in words ($r = .33$) was low. This would be expected since these items discriminate among older children who make higher scores on this test.

Inter-correlations of all tests in the Observation Survey were calculated for a New Zealand representative sample of 796 children aged five to seven years in 2000. In the United Kingdom, the inter-correlations among tasks were computed on a sample of 967 five to seven year-old children in 2009. The correlation coefficients for the New Zealand and United Kingdom studies based on the full samples and by age level are on pages 172–173. The correlations vary depending on age of the children and among tasks, with the range from .48 to .95 for the full samples (the full sample correlations likely yield the most accurate estimates of the true relationships among the tasks because those values are less influenced by non-normality in the subscore distributions that tend to occur at specific age levels). The inter-correlations among task scores are all relatively large and indicate good communality among the subscores. Furthermore, the correlation values taken together are not excessively high, revealing that each task contributes uniquely to understanding a student's literacy acquisition. Across the two studies, no task stands out as being considerably more or less correlated with the other tasks.

Besides examining the correlations among the tasks, research has been conducted to assess the degree to which task scores converge with other measures of literacy.

Gómez-Bellengé, Rodgers, Schulz, and Wang (2005) correlated subtest scores on the Iowa Test of Basic Skills (ITBS) with Observation Survey subscores from 242 first-grade children in the United States during the 2002–2003 school year. Correlations ranged from .21 to .80 with a mean of .49. The lowest correlations were for Letter Identification, which tends to be positively skewed, even by the fall of first grade. For the other Observation Survey tasks, the lowest correlations with any ITBS subtest were about .35. These values indicate a solid relationship between the ITBS and Survey tasks.

Holliman, Hurry, and Douëtil (2010) examined the correlations between Observation Survey tasks (except Text Level) and a portion of the Primary Reading Test and the British Spelling Test Series for a sample of 125 five- to seven-year-old children in the United Kingdom near the end of the 2008–2009 school year. The correlations for the full sample were all above .50 and were as high as .80 between the Duncan Word test and the British Spelling Test Series, reflecting solid convergence with the two other measures of literacy. D'Agostino (2012) correlated scores from the six Survey tasks with scores from the Slosson Oral Reading Test — Revised from a 2010–2011 United States sample of over 1,200 first-grade students at the beginning, middle and end of the school year. The correlations varied from .23 to .87, with the lowest value for Letter Identification at mid-year and the end of year, and the largest value for Text Reading Level in the beginning of the year. Most of the correlations were in the .50 range, indicating good convergence with the Slosson.

Predictive validity: A longitudinal follow-up study of Clay's (1966) original sample reported on the 83 children at 6.0 who remained in the same schools. Scores on two standardised Word Reading tests, Schonell R1 and Fieldhouse Reading Test (New Zealand Council for Educational Research) at seven and eight years were correlated with literacy and behaviour measures at six years. The correlations indicate how well the Clay-Schonell Word Reading Test (after one year at school) related to progress one and two years later. (Reported in Clay, 1979, 1985, 1991, page 207.)

Correlations of Reading Progress at 6:0
With Later Status on Standardised Tests at 7:0 and 8:0 Years

	Clay-Schonell 6:0	Schonell 7:0	8:0	Fieldhouse 7:0	8:0
	Concurrent Correlations	Predictive Correlations			
Clay Word Reading		.90	.80	.88	.83
Text Reading Accuracy	.93	.80	.69	.77	.72
Letter Identification	.84	.86	.81	.80	.83
Concepts About Print	.79	.73	.64	.69	.70
Error rate on text	.85	.78	.77		
Self-correction on text	.67	.61	.60		
Metropolitan Readiness	.55	.49	.45	.43	.48
Stanford-Binet I.Q.	.55	.54	.48	.50	.55

Reliability estimates

Since 1967, reliability coefficients for the Observation Survey tasks have often been reported for internal consistency, test-retest reliability, and inter-rater correlations. All Survey tasks have alternate forms to reduce practice effects when children are retested, except for Letter Identification which tests the entire set of symbols used in English each time. The reliability of the scores depends on standard procedures being used, and training in administration of the Observation Survey is essential. A sample of reliability coefficients for each task follows.

Author(s)	Date	Number of Children	Type of Reliability	Reliability	Reference	Location
Concepts About Print						
Clay	1966	100	Split half	.95	Clay, 1993b	NZ
Clay	1968	40	KR-20	.85	Clay, 1993b	NZ
Day & Day	1980	56	Split half	.84–.88	Day and Day, 1980	US
Perkins	1978		Test-retest	.73–.89	Perkins, 1978	US
Gilmore	1998		Alpha	.87	Min. of Ed., 1998	NZ
Pinnell, et al	1990	106	Alpha	.78	Clay, 1993b	US
Holliman, et al	2009	128	Test-retest	.91	Holliman, et al, 2010	UK
Holliman, et al	2009	112	Alpha	.83	Holliman, et al, 2010	UK
D'Agostino	2008	326	Alpha	.69	D'Agostino, 2012	US
Letter Identification						
Clay	1966	100	Split half	.97	Clay, 1993b	NZ
Pinnell, et al	1990	107	Alpha	.95	Clay, 1993b	US
Holliman, et al	2009	128	Test-retest	.96	Holliman, et al, 2010	UK
Holliman, et al	2009	112	Alpha	.94	Holliman, et al, 2010	UK
D'Agostino	2008	324	Alpha	.92	D'Agostino, 2012	US

Word Reading (Clay, Clay Word Test; Pinnell et al & D'Agostino, Ohio Word Test; Holliman et al, Duncan Word Test)

Clay	1966	100	KR-20	.90	Clay, 1993b	NZ
Pinnell, et al	1990	107	Alpha	.92	Clay, 1993b	US
Holliman, et al	2009	128	Test-retest	.96	Holliman, et al, 2010	UK
Holliman, et al	2009	112	Alpha	.96	Holliman, et al, 2010	UK
D'Agostino	2008	326	Alpha	.87	D'Agostino, 2012	US

Writing Vocabulary

Robinson	1972	34	Test-retest	.97	Clay, 1993b	NZ
Pinnell, et al	1994	107	Test-retest	.62	Clay, 1993b	US
Denton, et al		24	Inter-rater	.93	Denton, et al, 2006	US
Holliman, et al	2009	128	Test-retest	.92	Holliman, et al, 2010	UK

Hearing and Recording Sounds in Words

Clay	1979	160	Test-retest	.64	Clay, 1979	NZ
Pinnell, et al	1990	107	Alpha	.96	Pinnell, et al, 1990	US
Pinnell, et al	1994	403	Split half	.84–.88	Pinnell, et al, 1994	US
Holliman, et al	2009	128	Test-retest	.93	Holliman, et al, 2010	UK
Holliman, et al	2009	112	Alpha	.95	Holliman, et al 2010	UK
D'Agostino	2008	316	Alpha	.92	D'Agostino, 2012	US

Text Reading Level

Denton, et al		24	Inter-rater	.98	Denton, et al, 2006	US
D'Agostino	2008	293	Test-retest	.96	D'Agostino, 2012	US

The reliability of recording and scoring Running Records

In Clay's dissertation research (1966) taped recordings of five-year-old children reading were taken for four children over the period of one year. These were used to check on the reliability of a trained observer's recording and scoring of error rates and self-correction rates with two years' interval between the two analyses ($r = .98$ for error scoring and $r = .68$ for self-correction rate). Inter-rater reliability was established as follows. After one hour of training, five graduate students scored 12 reading observations selected at random from the taped recordings of the original reading sessions with two children ranked 94th and 76th in the final test of reading progress (high = 100). Chi-square tests yielded no significant differences at the .01 level for the raters' recording and scoring of error and self-correction behaviours.

A number of trends became obvious during these reliability tests.

- For beginning readers, observers can take Running Records which give reliable accuracy scores with a small amount of training.

- The effect of poor observation is to reduce the number of errors recorded and increase the accuracy rate. As the observer's skill in recording at speed increases, so the error scores tend to rise.

- To record all error behaviour in full, as against merely tallying its occurrence, takes much more practice (but provides more evidence of the child's processing strengths).

- Observations for poor readers require longer training to reach agreement on scoring standards because of the complex error behaviour.

- Information is lost on taped observation, especially motor behaviour and visual survey, but observation of vocal behaviour tends to be improved.

- Reliability probably drops as reading accuracy level falls because there is more behaviour to be recorded in the same time span.

For research work the most reliable records would be obtained by scoring an observation immediately following its manual recording and rechecking immediately with a taped observation (Clay, 1993b, page 28).

Validity and reliability data for the Spanish Observation Survey

Escamilla (1992) prepared a report for the Office of Educational Research and Improvement (OERI) on a grant provided by the OERI Fellows Program in 1991–1992.

Concurrent validity: Each task of the Spanish Observation Survey was correlated to the Aprenda Total Reading Score (Nivel Preprimario) for N = 202–282 children sampled at three sites: Tucson, Chicago and Texas.

The resulting correlations are as follows:

	Fall	Spring
Concepts About Print (CAP)	.53	.51
Letter Identification (LI)	.60	.66
Word Reading (WR)	.72	.75
Writing Vocabulary (WV)	.66	.65
Hearing and Recording Sounds in Words (HRSW)	.70	.60

The author considered these coefficients to be adequate to establish the concurrent validity of this instrument (Escamilla, 1992, page 22). To assess construct and/or internal validity of the Survey as a whole she reported inter-correlations between the Spanish Observation Survey tasks for all sites for fall and spring testing.

Fall 1991

	LI	WR	CAP	WV
LI				
WR	.71			
CAP	.53	.62		
WV	.73	.87	.63	
HRSW	.83	.82	.61	.82

Spring 1992

	LI	WR	CAP	WV
LI				
WR	.78			
CAP	.64	.66		
WV	.72	.83	.60	
HRSW	.84	.86	.68	.79

Escamilla concluded that these results indicate that there is a positive inter-relationship among the various observation tasks on the Spanish Observation Survey.

Spanish Observation Survey Reliability Estimates

Observation Task	Number of children	Type of reliability	Reliability Fall	Spring
Concepts About Print	282/202	Cronbach Alpha	.69	.82
Letter Identification	"	Cronbach Alpha	.94	.96
Word Reading	"	Cronbach Alpha	.95	.97
Writing Vocabulary	"	Test-retest	.87	.89
Hearing and Recording Sounds in Words	"	Cronbach Alpha	.96	.95

Inter-correlations among tasks by age group

The tables below display inter-correlations among Observation Survey tasks found in separate analyses conducted in New Zealand (2000) and the United Kingdom (Holliman et al, 2010). The results are displayed for all students in the norming sample as well as for subsets of students identified by Age Group (i.e., 5.00-5.50, 5.51-6.0, 6.01-6.50, 6.51-7.0).

To locate the correlations between tasks resulting from the New Zealand analyses read the cells above (or to the right of) the diagonal created by the 1.000 correlations. To locate correlations between tasks resulting from the analyses of data collected in the United Kingdom, read the cells below (or to the left of) the diagonal created by the 1.000 correlations. (Note that neither Text Level nor Word Reading scores were included in the United Kingdom analyses.)

Inter-correlations among Observation Survey tasks (upper diagonal—NZ norming study, total sample, N = 796; lower diagonal—Holliman et al 2010 UK study, total sample, N = 967)

	TL	LI	CAP	WR	WV	HRSW	DUN
TL	1.000	.554	.768	.877	.885	.804	.859
LI	–	1.000	.681	.691	.575	.799	.737
CAP	–	.594	1.000	.759	.761	.792	.764
WR	–	–	–	1.000	.839	.894	.945
WV	–	.501	.682	–	1.000	.811	.831
HRSW	–	.720	.692	–	.638	1.000	.921
DUN	–	.694	.777	–	.697	.804	1.000

Inter-correlations for Age Group: 5.00 – 5.50 Years (upper diagonal—NZ norming study, N = 223; lower diagonal—Holliman et al 2010 UK study, N = 254)

	TL	LI	CAP	WR	WV	HRSW	DUN
TL	1.00	.48	.59	.59	.59	.71	.81
LI	–	1.00	.68	.63	.61	.76	.66
CAP	–	.48	1.00	.64	.66	.73	.68
WR	–	–	–	1.00	.88	.84	.93
WV	–	.51	.44	–	1.00	.85	.88
HRSW	–	.66	.58	–	.64	1.00	.87
DUN	–	.66	.61	–	.66	.72	1.00

Inter-correlations for Age Group: 5.51 – 6.00 Years (upper diagonal—NZ norming study, N = 170; lower diagonal—Holliman et al 2010 UK study, N = 251)

	TL	LI	CAP	WR	WV	HRSW	DUN
TL	1.00	.47	.64	.84	.84	.74	.83
LI	–	1.00	.62	.61	.55	.76	.69
CAP	–	.65	1.00	.64	.66	.74	.68
WR	–	–	–	1.00	.82	.82	.91
WV	–	.50	.60	–	1.00	.82	.85
HRSW	–	.71	.67	–	.62	1.00	.88
DUN	–	.68	.76	–	.68	.76	1.00

Inter-correlations for Age Group: 6.01 – 6.50 Years (upper diagonal—NZ norming study, N = 230; lower diagonal—Holliman et al 2010 UK study, N = 248)

	TL	LI	CAP	WR	WV	HRSW	DUN
TL	1.00	.49	.75	.85	.82	.76	.81
LI	–	1.00	.61	.65	.49	.78	.73
CAP	–	.40	1.00	.69	.70	.69	.70
WR	–	–	–	1.00	.75	.84	.90
WV	–	.33	.56	–	1.00	.74	.74
HRSW	–	.46	.53	–	.51	1.00	.89
DUN	–	.50	.67	–	.51	.71	1.00

Inter-correlations for Age Group: 6.51 – 7.00 Years (upper diagonal—NZ norming study, N = 173; lower diagonal—Holliman et al 2010 UK study, N = 224)

	TL	LI	CAP	WR	WV	HRSW	DUN
TL	1.00	.54	.68	.78	.78	.76	.76
LI	–	1.00	.56	.75	.48	.83	.80
CAP	–	.48	1.00	.62	.65	.65	.60
WR	–	–	–	1.00	.68	.87	.90
WV	–	.38	.62	–	1.00	.68	.64
HRSW	–	.64	.54	–	.48	1.00	.89
DUN	–	.64	.65	–	.53	.73	1.00

Appendix 3

New Zealand norms for the Observation Survey

The sample and testing

The cooperation of several groups made it possible to conduct a national normative study in New Zealand in the year 2000. The research division of the Ministry of Education selected a representative sample of schools across the country and 35 Reading Recovery Tutors and Trainers assessed four children selected at random from the five to seven year age groups in each school. Complete data, full Observation Surveys, were obtained for 796 children from 199 schools (four from each school). The characteristics of the sample in terms of child gender and age group are displayed in the following table.

Sample: Age Group (in years) by Gender

Gender	5.00–5.50	5.51–6.00	6.01–6.50	6.51–7.00	Totals
Females	104	92	130	84	410
Males	119	78	100	89	386
Totals	223	170	230	173	796

Tabled information

The results were checked and collated by Reading Recovery Trainers at the Auckland College of Education and the results were analysed independently by Dr Ken Rowe, Principal Researcher at the Australian Council for Educational Research in Melbourne, Australia. Rowe made a strong recommendation from the data collected to discard the five to seven year stanine grouping used previously and adopt stanines for six-monthly age groups. In simple terms this is because, as the histograms on page 175 show, large amounts of change occur during the first two years of formal schooling and the timing of those changes is different on different tasks. Norms which apply across a two-year time span are no longer satisfactory. It is more appropriate to compare each child with a group who have been at school for a similar period of time. When consulting the New Zealand stanine tables it is important to remember that New Zealand children enter school on their fifth birthday.

The graphs which show change over time across the four age groups provide important information for the design of research or assessment for the early years of school. Stanines are reported so that teachers can consider the progress of individuals across a profile of scores, but included are the percentile tables for researchers and those engaged in studies of subgroups of children because percentiles are to be valued more when interpreting group trends.

These technical notes may assist other education authorities to obtain Observation Survey information on their own school populations. The tough questions are 'With whom do you wish to compare the individual children you wish to assess?' and 'For what purpose would you make this comparison?'

Graphs of score distributions by age group

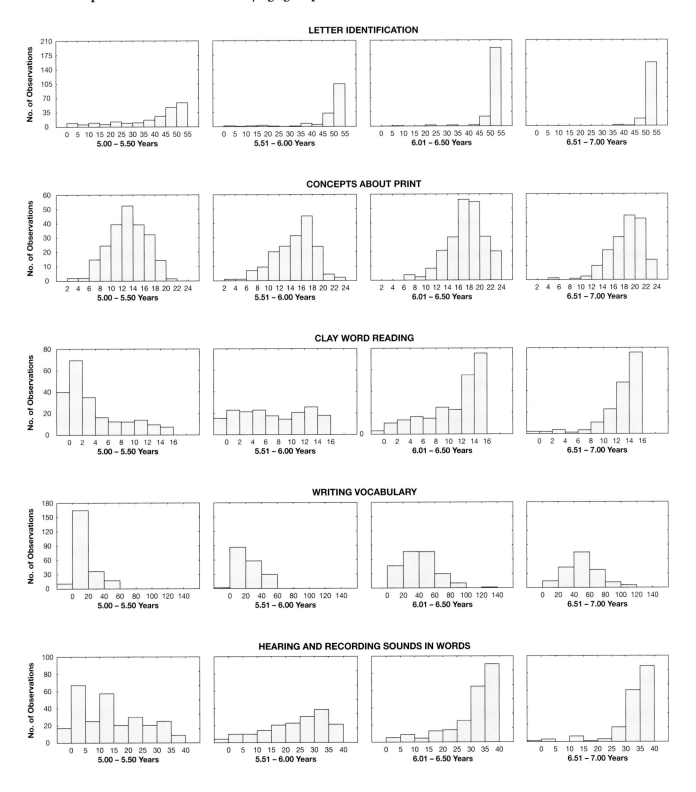

Box-and-whisker plots for tasks by age group

The following graphs are 'box-and-whisker' plots for each of the Observation Survey tasks (by age group). The graphs show significant change over time. They:

- describe the distribution of raw scores for the 'middle' 50 percent of the cases (bounded by the 75th and 25th percentile values, respectively), with non-outlier minimum and maximum score values indicated by 'whiskers'

- indicate the mean, surrounded by box-values of ±1 standard deviation (SD), and bounded by 95% confidence intervals (represented by the 'whiskers').

Box plots for *Letter Identification*

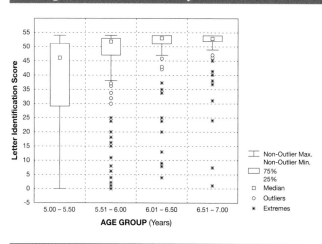

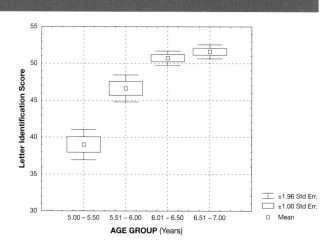

Box plots for *Concepts About Print*

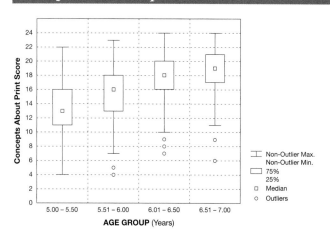

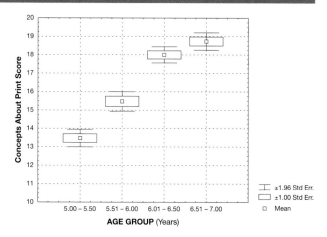

The graphs above (left) describe the 'shape' of the score distribution for four age groups.

The graphs above (right) indicate that there are significant differences among the score means for the four age groups (at the 0.05 α level), since their respective 95% confidence intervals do not overlap.

Box plots for *Clay Word Reading*

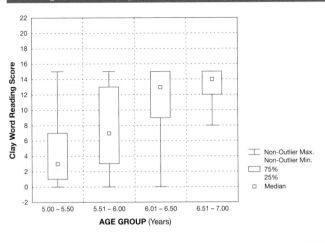

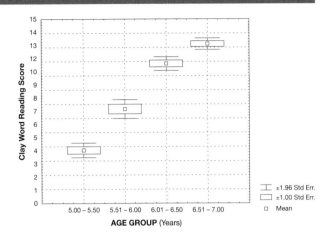

Box plots for *Writing Vocabulary*

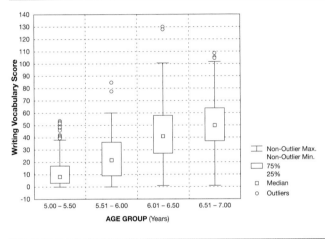

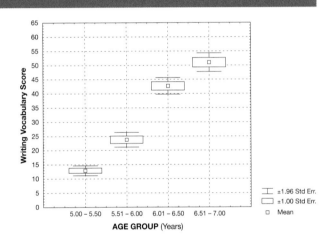

Box plots for *Hearing and Recording Sounds in Words*

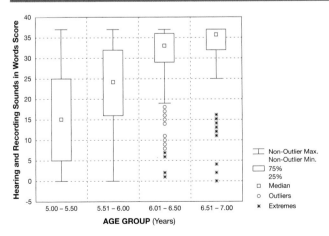

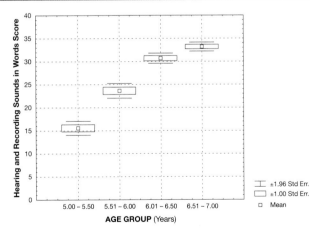

The graphs above (left) describe the 'shape' of the score distribution for four age groups.

The graphs above (right) indicate that there are significant differences among the score means for the four age groups (at the 0.05 α level), since their respective 95% confidence intervals do not overlap.

Observation Survey age group profiles across tasks: percentile ranks and stanines

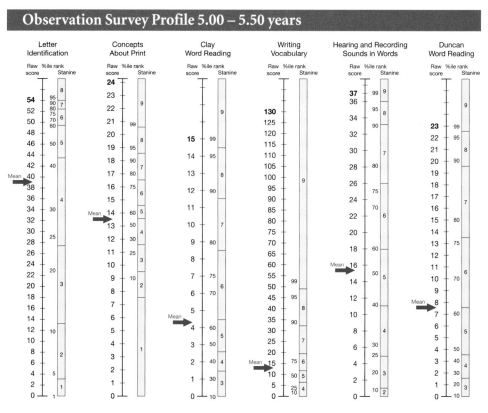

Observation Survey Profile 5.00 – 5.50 years

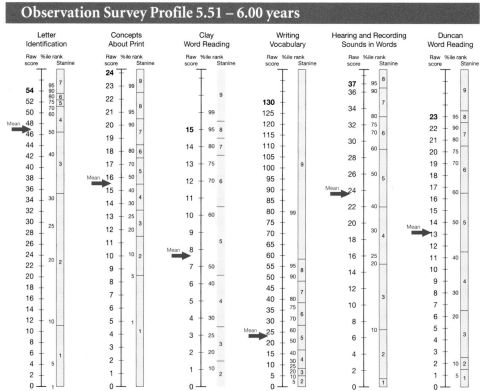

Observation Survey Profile 5.51 – 6.00 years

Observation Survey Profile 6.01 – 6.50 years

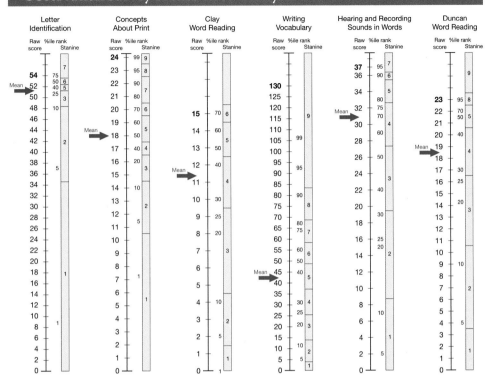

Observation Survey Profile 6.51 – 7.00 years

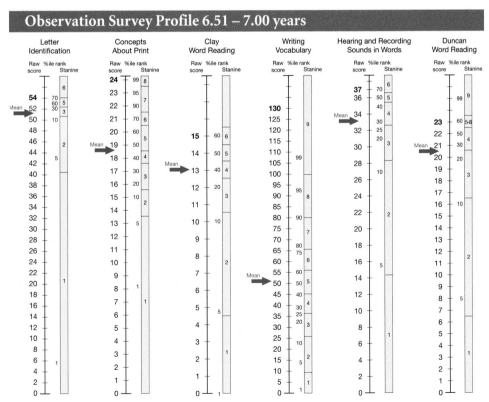

Appendix 4

Canadian norms for the Observation Survey

Huggins, I., Matczuk, A., Tolentino, J. and Kniskern, J. (2008). *Developing Canadian Norms for An Observation Survey of Early Literacy Achievement*. Canadian Institute of Reading Recovery (Western Division).

The sample and testing

To establish the Canadian norms, a national random sample of first-grade students from four provinces (Manitoba, Nova Scotia, Ontario, Prince Edward Island) and the Yukon Territory was identified in schools implementing Reading Recovery during the 2006–2007 academic year. Students were eligible for selection if they were in grade one and were receiving their language arts instruction in English. Students were included regardless of special learning needs or programs, including participation in Reading Recovery. The selection process was completed by Reading Recovery teachers who randomly identified two first-grade students in their schools. In total, 1010 random sample students were tested at three points during the academic year (fall or the beginning of the year, mid-year, year-end).

Tabled information

Following are the resulting summary statistics and score distribution graphs for five tasks, Letter Identification, Word Reading, Concepts About Print, Writing Vocabulary, and Hearing and Recording Sounds in Words.

Letter Identification

Letter Identification Summary Statistics					
Period	N	Range	Median	Mean	SD
Fall	1006	1–54	51	47.16	9.34
Mid-Year	965	18–54	53	52.53	2.63
Year-End	943	11–54	54	53.33	1.89

Letter Identification Distribution of Scores

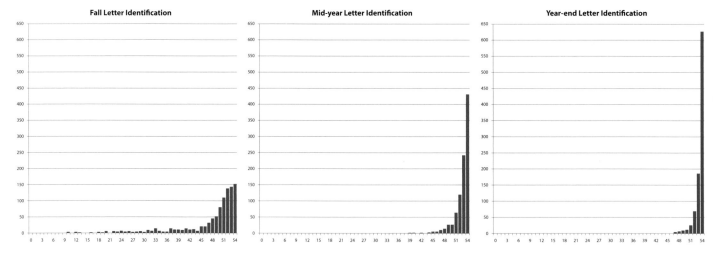

Word Reading

Word Reading Summary Statistics					
Period	**N**	**Range**	**Median**	**Mean**	**SD**
Fall	1005	0–15	4	6.01	5.05
Mid-Year	967	0–15	13	11.97	3.55
Year-End	943	0–15	15	13.72	2.19

Word Reading Distribution of Scores

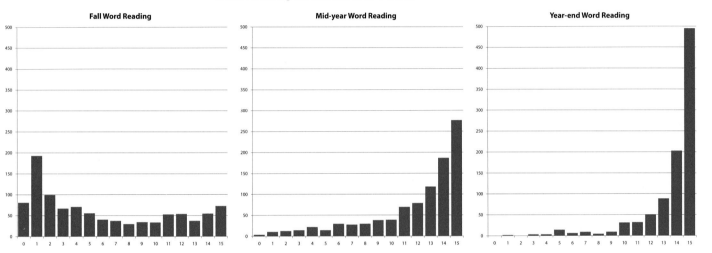

Concepts About Print

Concepts About Print Summary Statistics					
Period	**N**	**Range**	**Median**	**Mean**	**SD**
Fall	1005	0–24	14	13.78	4.75
Mid-Year	967	0–24	19	18.63	3.40
Year-End	943	2–24	21	20.72	2.81

Concepts About Print Distribution of Scores

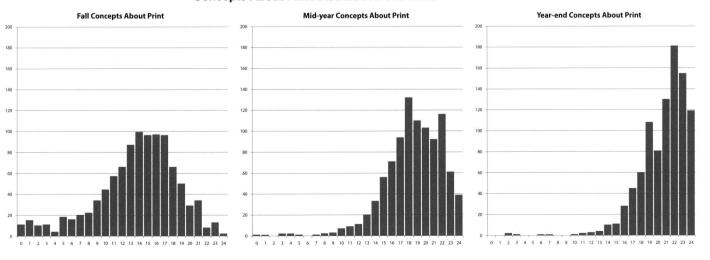

Writing Vocabulary

Writing Vocabulary Summary Statistics					
Period	N	Range	Median	Mean	SD
Fall	1006	0–82	11	13.98	11.70
Mid-Year	967	1–104	34	35.36	16.24
Year-End	943	3–126	48	48.56	18.15

Writing Vocabulary Distribution of Scores

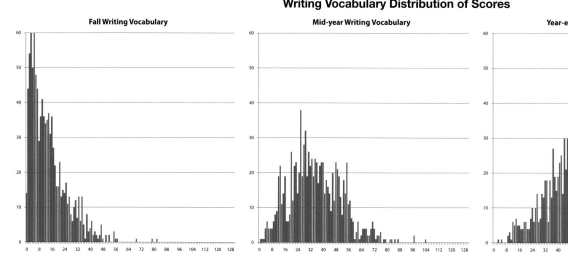
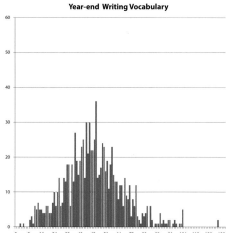

Hearing and Recording Sounds in Words

Hearing and Recording Sounds in Words Summary Statistics					
Period	N	Range	Median	Mean	SD
Fall	1005	0–37	23	21.55	10.79
Mid-Year	967	1–37	35	32.70	5.69
Year-End	943	9–37	36	35.09	3.40

Hearing and Recording Sounds in Words Distribution of Scores

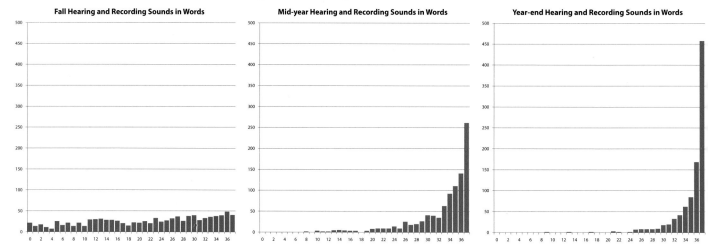

Appendix 5

United Kingdom (England and Wales) norms for the Observation Survey

Holliman, A.J., Hurry, J. and Douëtil, J. (2010). *Standardisation of the Observation Survey in England and Wales, UK.* University of London, London: Institute of Education.

The sample and testing

A systematic random procedure was used to invite a subset of schools drawn from a random stratified sample of 300 schools identified by the National Foundation for Educational Research as representative of the wider population of schools in England and Wales on the basis of government office region, percentage eligible for free school meals, and school locale. This process resulted in identification of 69 schools agreeing to participate in the standardisation study. To secure the participants for this study, a systematic random sampling procedure was used to select two boys and two girls from each of four age ranges in each school. The ranges, in years, are: 5.00 – 5.50; 5.51 – 6.00; 6.01 – 6.50; 6.51 – 7.00. Reading Recovery children were not included due to their familiarity with the assessments. It is also noted that for a very small sample of schools, the random selection process had to be abandoned due to too few participants matching the selection criteria.

A subsequent comparison of the sample's demographic characteristics (i.e., gender, ethnicity, first language, eligibility for free school meals) confirmed that the 980 participating children were similar to the population data from the 2009 census reported by the Department for Children, Schools and Families. (See Holliman, Hurry & Douëtil for complete detail of demographic characteristics.)

Observation Survey testing was completed at the end of the 2008–2009 school year in June and July, and all testing was conducted by individuals trained to administer the Observation Survey. The following tasks were administered and standardised: Letter Identification, Concepts About Print, Duncan Word Test, Writing Vocabulary, and Hearing and Recording Sounds in Words. The stanines and percentile ranks were calculated for each task, for each of the four age groups. Further technical details are provided in the full report (Holliman et al, 2010).

Tabled information

On the following pages are the stanines, percentile ranks and score distributions for the Observation Survey tasks for the four age ranges of children. Stanines and summary statistics are also found in the stanine tables.

Stanine and percentile ranks for 5.00 – 5.50 years (for 254 children in 2009)

Letter Identification (N = 254)			Concept About Print (N = 254)			Duncan Word Test (N = 254)			Writing Vocabulary (N = 250)			HRSW (N = 250)		
Raw	Stan.	Perc.	Raw	Stan.	Perc.	Raw	Stan.	Perc.	Raw	Stan.	Perc.	Raw	Stan.	Perc.
0-11	1	0	0-2	1	0	0	2	6	0	2	4	0-1	1	2
12-15	1	1	3	1	2	1	2	10	1	2	8	2	2	4
16-18	1	2	4-5	1	3	2	3	15	2	3	12	3	2	6
19-23	1	3	6	2	5	3	3	19	3	3	18	4	2	8
24-25	2	4	7	2	10	4	4	25	4	4	23	5	2	9
26-27	2	5	8	3	14	5	4	31	5	4	28	6	3	11
28-29	2	7	9	4	23	6	4	35	6	4	33	7	3	12
30	2	10	10	4	26	7	4	39	7	4	36	8	3	14
31-32	3	11	11	4	37	8	5	44	8	5	40	9	3	17
33	3	12	12	5	49	9	5	49	9	5	44	10	3	18
34	3	13	13	6	61	10	5	55	10	5	48	11	3	21
35	3	14	14	6	71	11	5	59	11	5	52	12	4	24
36	3	15	15	7	79	12	6	66	12	5	57	13	4	25
37	3	17	16	7	87	13	6	70	13	6	60	14	4	28
38	3	18	17	8	92	14	6	76	14	6	66	15	4	29
39	3	20	18	9	96	15	7	79	15	6	68	16	4	32
40	3	21	19-20	9	98	16	7	81	16	6	71	17	4	33
41	3	22	21-24	9	99	17	7	83	17	6	74	18	4	34
42	4	24				18	7	85	18	6	76	19	4	36
43	4	26				19	7	88	19	7	78	20	4	39
44	4	29				20	8	90	20	7	80	21	5	40
45	4	33				21	8	93	21	7	83	22	5	42
46	4	38				22	9	97	22	7	84	23	5	46
47	5	43				23	9	99	23	7	87	24	5	49
48	5	52							24	7	88	25	5	52
49	5	59							25	8	89	26	5	55
50	6	68							26	8	90	27	5	58
51	7	77							27	8	91	28	6	63
52	7	88							28	8	92	29	6	66
53	9	97							29-30	8	94	30	6	70
54	9	99							31-33	9	96	31	6	74
									34-37	9	97	32	7	78
									38-44	9	98	33	7	83
									45+	9	99	34	7	88
												35	8	92
												36	9	97
												37	9	99

Note: Raw = Raw Score; Stan. = Stanine; Perc. = Percentile Rank; HRSW = Hearing and Recording Sounds in Words (also known as Dictation).

Stanine and percentile ranks for 5.51 – 6.00 years (for 251 children in 2009)

Letter Identification (N = 251)		
Raw	Stan.	Perc.
0-9	1	0
10-19	1	1
20-23	1	2
24	1	3
25-26	2	4
27-30	2	5
31-34	2	6
35-37	2	7
38-40	2	8
41	2	10
42	3	11
43	3	13
44	3	16
45	3	17
46	3	19
47	4	23
48	4	26
49	4	29
50	5	40
51	5	55
52	6	70
53	7	86
54	8-9	99

Concept About Print (N = 251)		
Raw	Stan.	Perc.
0-3	1	1
4-5	1	2
6	1	3
7	2	6
8	2	8
9	3	12
10	3	14
11	3	18
12	4	25
13	4	30
14	5	40
15	5	51
16	5	59
17	6	71
18	7	77
19	7	88
20	8	91
21	9	96
22-23	9	98
24	9	99

Duncan Word Test (N = 249)		
Raw	Stan.	Perc.
0	2	4
1	2	7
2	2	9
3	2	10
4	3	12
5	3	14
6	3	16
7	3	19
8	3	20
9	4	23
10	4	25
11	4	29
12	4	32
13	4	35
14	4	37
15	5	41
16	5	43
17	5	47
18	5	53
19	5	56
20	6	62
21	6	71
22	7	83
23	8-9	99

Writing Vocabulary (N = 249)		
Raw	Stan.	Perc.
0	2	4
1	2	6
2-3	2	8
4	2	9
5	3	11
6	3	12
7	3	14
8	3	18
9	3	20
10	4	23
11	4	24
12	4	27
13	4	29
14	4	33
15	4	34
16	4	39
17	5	42
18	5	47
19	5	51
20	5	52
21	5	55
22	5	56
23	5	59
24	6	61
25	6	63
26	6	65
27	6	66
28	6	67
29	6	69
30	6	71
31	6	74
32	6	76
33	7	77
34	7	79
35	7	82
36	7	84
37	7	86
38	7	87
39	7	88
40	8	89
41-42	8	90
43	8	93
44-46	8	94
47-51	8	95
52-55	9	96
56	9	97
57-67	9	98
68+	9	99

HRSW (N = 248)		
Raw	Stan.	Perc.
0	1	1
1	1	2
2	1	3
3-6	2	4
7	2	5
8-9	2	8
10	2	9
11	3	11
12-14	3	12
15	3	13
16	3	14
17	3	15
18	3	17
19	3	19
20-21	3	20
22	3	21
23	4	23
24	4	26
25	4	27
26	4	29
27	4	31
28	4	34
29	4	36
30	5	42
31	5	46
32	5	52
33	5	57
34	6	67
35	6	76
36	7	85
37	8-9	99

Note: Raw = Raw Score; Stan. = Stanine; Perc. = Percentile Rank; HRSW = Hearing and Recording Sounds in Words (also known as Dictation).

Stanine and percentile ranks for 6.01 – 6.50 years (for 248 children in 2009)

Letter Identification (N = 248)			Concept About Print (N = 249)			Duncan Word Test (N = 247)			Writing Vocabulary (N = 250)			HRSW (N = 250)		
Raw	Stan.	Perc.	Raw	Stan.	Perc.	Raw	Stan.	Perc.	Raw	Stan.	Perc.	Raw	Stan.	Perc.
0-39	1	0	0-8	1	0	0-3	1	0	0-3	1	0	0-17	1	0
40	1	1	9	1	2	4-5	1	1	4-6	1	1	18	1	1
41-43	1	2	10	2	4	6-7	1	2	7	1	2	19-21	1	2
44	1	3	11	2	5	8	1	3	8	1	3	22-23	1	3
45	2	4	12	2	9	9	2	5	9	2	4	24-25	2	4
46	2	6	13	3	14	10	2	6	10-11	2	7	26	2	6
47	2	9	14	3	18	11	2	8	12	2	8	27-28	2	7
48	3	12	15	4	26	12	2	10	13	2	10	29	3	11
49	3	19	16	4	36	13	3	13	14	3	13	30	3	15
50	4	27	17	5	48	14	3	16	15	3	14	31	3	19
51	4	34	18	6	62	15	3	19	16	3	17	32	4	24
52	5	57	19	6	70	16	3	21	17	3	19	33	4	30
53	7	77	20	6	76	17	4	25	18	3	22	34	4	37
54	8-9	99	21	7	85	18	4	29	19	4	24	35	5	50
			22	8	92	19	4	32	20	4	29	36	6	68
			23	9	98	20	4	37	21	4	32	37	7-9	99
			24	9	99	21	5	43	22	4	35			
						22	6	60	23	4	38			
						23	7-9	99	24	5	43			
									25	5	45			
									26	5	50			
									27-28	5	52			
									29	5	54			
									30	5	55			
									31	5	58			
									32	6	61			
									33	6	63			
									34	6	67			
									35	6	69			
									36	6	72			
									37	6	73			
									38	6	74			
									39	6	76			
									40	7	78			
									41	7	79			
									42	7	82			
									43	7	83			
									44	7	84			
									45-46	7	87			
									47-48	7	88			
									49	8	89			
									50	8	90			
									51-54	8	91			
									55	8	92			
									56-57	8	93			
									58	8	94			
									59	8	95			
									60	9	96			
									61-62	9	97			
									63-75	9	98			
									76+	9	99			

Note: Raw = Raw Score; Stan. = Stanine; Perc. = Percentile Rank; HRSW = Hearing and Recording Sounds in Words (also known as Dictation).

Stanine and percentile ranks for 6.51 – 7.00 years (for 224 children in 2009)

Letter Identification (N = 224)			Concept About Print (N = 224)			Duncan Word Test (N = 224)			Writing Vocabulary (N = 224)			HRSW (N = 223)		
Raw	Stan.	Perc.	Raw	Stan.	Perc.	Raw	Stan.	Perc.	Raw	Stan.	Perc.	Raw	Stan.	Perc.
0-35	1	0	0-8	1	0	0-2	1	0	0-5	1	0	0-8	1	0
36-41	1	1	9-10	1	1	3-6	1	1	6-7	1	2	9-12	1	1
42	1	2	11	1	2	7	1	2	8	1	3	13-19	1	2
43-44	1	3	12	2	4	8	1	3	9-10	2	4	20-21	1	3
45	2	4	13	2	6	9-10	2	4	11-12	2	5	22-23	2	4
46	2	5	14	2	8	11	2	6	13	2	6	24	2	5
47	2	6	15	3	14	12-13	2	7	14	2	7	25-26	2	6
48	2	8	16	3	20	14	2	8	15	2	8	27-28	2	7
49	3	12	17	4	30	15	2	10	16	2	10	29	2	8
50	3	18	18	5	41	16	3	11	17-18	3	12	30	2	9
51	4	28	19	5	52	17	3	12	19	3	15	31	3	13
52	4	39	20	6	63	18	3	15	20	3	16	32	3	16
53	6	69	21	6	75	19	3	18	21	3	18	33	3	19
54	7-9	99	22	7	87	20	4	23	22	3	21	34	4	25
			23	8	92	21	4	31	23-24	4	25	35	4	34
			24	9	99	22	5	45	25	4	28	36	5	49
						23	6-9	99	26	4	31	37	6-9	99
									27	4	33			
									28	4	34			
									29	4	36			
									30	5	41			
									31-32	5	42			
									33	5	44			
									34	5	46			
									35	5	47			
									36	5	51			
									37	5	54			
									38	5	56			
									39	5	58			
									40	6	62			
									41	6	64			
									42	6	66			
									43	6	67			
									44	6	70			
									45	6	71			
									46	6	72			
									47	6	73			
									48	6	75			
									49	7	78			
									50	7	79			
									51	7	82			
									52	7	83			
									53	7	84			
									54	7	86			
									55-57	7	87			
									58	7	88			
									59	8	89			
									60-61	8	90			
									62	8	92			
									63	8	93			
									64	8	94			
									65-67	8	95			
									68-69	9	96			
									70-71	9	97			
									72-76	9	98			
									77+	9	99			

Note: Raw = Raw Score; Stan. = Stanine; Perc. = Percentile Rank; HRSW = Hearing and Recording Sounds in Words (also known as Dictation).

Score distributions by age group

LETTER IDENTIFICATION

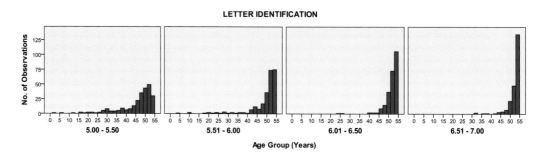

CONCEPTS ABOUT PRINT

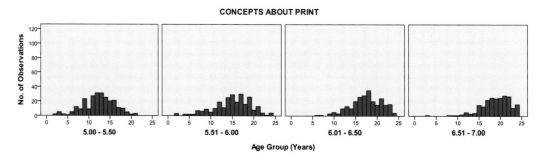

DUNCAN WORD TEST

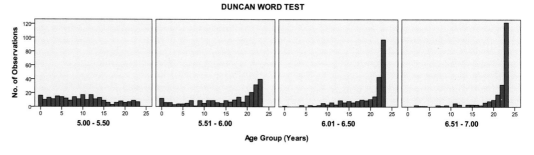

WRITING VOCABULARY

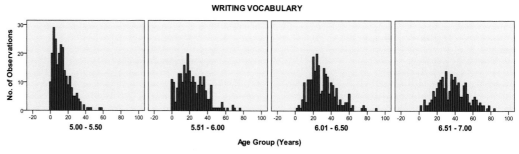

HEARING AND RECORDING SOUNDS IN WORDS

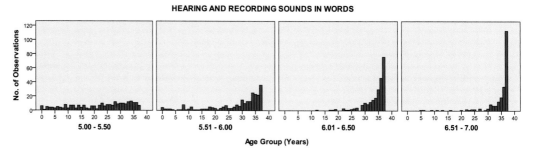

Appendix 6

United States norms for the Observation Survey

D'Agostino, J.V. (2012). *US norms for tasks of An Observation Survey of Early Literacy Achievement.* Columbus, OH: The Ohio State University International Data Evaluation Center.

The sample

The norms for the United States are derived from test data on a random sample of first-grade students attending schools implementing Reading Recovery during the 2010–2011 academic year. The total number of participating schools was 4,688, or about nine percent of approximately 52,000 primary schools in the United States. Because schools were not chosen randomly to provide Reading Recovery, the 4,688 schools were not likely representative of schools throughout the country. Thus, the norms provided below are based on data from a subset representative of the schools that offer Reading Recovery nationally and are not considered a microcosm of American primary schools.

In each participating school, two children from first-grade classrooms participating in the Reading Recovery intervention were chosen randomly for the sample regardless of special services, including Reading Recovery instruction. These random sample children were tested with the Observation Survey at three points: beginning (fall), mid-year (December to February), and end of the school year (spring).

There were 8,716 random sample students who participated in the data collection, and it is noted that complete data were available for only one random sample participant in several participating schools. To conduct the analyses, it was determined important to weigh random sample students because only two students (or in some cases only one student) were chosen per school and because these schools varied in size, i.e., their first-grade enrolment numbers. This made it possible to consider the number of children each random sample student represented in his or her respective school.

Using the number of first-grade students at each participating Reading Recovery school in 2009–2010, sample weights were computed for each random sample student by dividing the total number of first-grade students in the school by the number of random sample students drawn from that school. Subsequently, the percentages of students according to ethnicity, gender, and eligibility for free and reduced lunch prices were computed for the weighted sample and compared to national statistics derived from the US Department of Education Common Core Data. The results revealed that about one tenth of US first-graders were in the sampled schools, and the demographics of the weighted random sample were similar to the national population of first-graders in many respects (see D'Agostino, 2012, for full detail of the demographic characteristics).

Tabled information

The following tables display the summary statistics for the weighted sample on each of the six tasks of the Observation Survey at three time points (fall, mid-year, and year end), the distribution of scores, and the national percentile ranks.

Letter Identification

Summary Statistics					
Period	N	Range	Median	Mean	SD
Fall	318,433	0–54	52	51.13	4.59
Mid-Year	299,678	4–54	54	53.03	2.16
Year-End	299,083	6–54	54	53.46	1.74

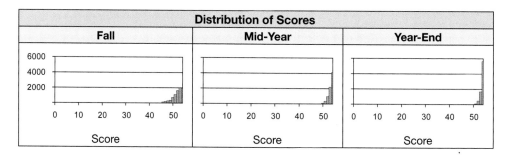

Distribution of Scores — Fall, Mid-Year, Year-End (Score vs. count)

National Percentile Ranks							
Raw Score	National Percentile Rank			Raw Score	National Percentile Rank		
	Fall	Mid-Year	Year-End		Fall	Mid-Year	Year-End
0-37	1	1	1	48	11	1	1
38-40	2	1	1	49	15	2	1
41-42	3	1	1	50	24	4	1
43	4	1	1	51	36	8	3
44-45	5	1	1	52	54	21	10
46	7	1	1	53	77	48	30
47	8	1	1	54	99	99	99

Concepts About Print

Summary Statistics					
Period	N	Range	Median	Mean	SD
Fall	318,092	1–24	15	15.08	3.49
Mid-Year	298,678	4–24	19	18.78	2.87
Year-End	299,023	3–24	21	20.74	2.50

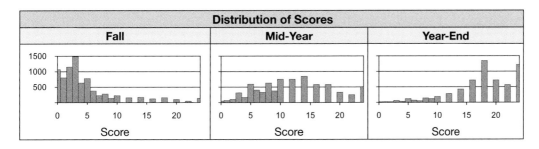

Distribution of Scores		
Fall	**Mid-Year**	**Year-End**

National Percentile Ranks

Raw Score	National Percentile Rank			Raw Score	National Percentile Rank			Raw Score	National Percentile Rank		
	Fall	Mid-Year	Year-End		Fall	Mid-Year	Year-End		Fall	Mid-Year	Year-End
0-6	1	1	1	13	28	4	1	20	95	70	39
7	2	1	1	14	40	7	2	21	97	81	54
8	4	1	1	15	52	12	3	22	98	91	73
9	6	1	1	16	64	19	6	23	99	96	89
10	9	1	1	17	76	30	9	24	99	99	99
11	14	1	1	18	85	44	17				
12	20	2	1	19	91	58	26				

Ohio Word Test

Summary Statistics

Period	N	Range	Median	Mean	SD
Fall	318,415	0–20	8	9.07	4.59
Mid-Year	298,660	0–20	18	16.11	4.25
Year-End	299,083	0–20	20	19.01	2.17

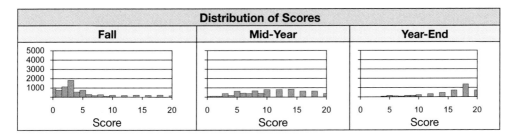

Distribution of Scores		
Fall	**Mid-Year**	**Year-End**

National Percentile Ranks

Raw Score	National Percentile Rank			Raw Score	National Percentile Rank			Raw Score	National Percentile Rank		
	Fall	Mid-Year	Year-End		Fall	Mid-Year	Year-End		Fall	Mid-Year	Year-End
0	4	1	1	7	49	5	1	14	74	28	3
1	9	1	1	8	54	7	1	15	78	34	5
2	15	1	1	9	59	9	1	16	81	41	7
3	22	1	1	10	62	12	1	17	84	49	11
4	29	1	1	11	65	15	1	18	88	59	19
5	36	2	1	12	69	19	2	19	93	72	37
6	43	3	1	13	72	23	2	20	99	99	99

Writing Vocabulary

Summary Statistics					
Period	N	Range	Median	Mean	SD
Fall	318,362	0–163	18	20.22	12.50
Mid-Year	298,692	0–126	42	42.95	15.78
Year-End	299,053	1–175	56	57.13	18.38

Distribution of Scores		
Fall	Mid-Year	Year-End

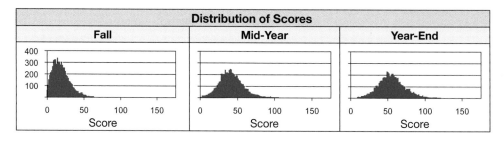

Raw Score	National Percentile Rank			Raw Score	National Percentile Rank			Raw Score	National Percentile Rank		
	Fall	Mid-Year	Year-End		Fall	Mid-Year	Year-End		Fall	Mid-Year	Year-End
0	1	1	1	31	83	23	6	62	99	89	64
1	1	1	1	32	85	25	7	63	99	90	66
2	2	1	1	33	86	27	8	64	99	91	69
3	3	1	1	34	87	29	9	65	99	92	71
4	5	1	1	35	89	33	10	66	99	92	73
5	8	1	1	36	90	35	11	67	99	93	74
6	10	1	1	37	91	38	12	68	99	94	76
7	13	1	1	38	92	40	14	69	99	94	77
8	16	1	1	39	92	43	15	70	99	94	79
9	20	1	1	40	93	46	16	71	99	95	80
10	23	1	1	41	94	48	18	72	99	95	81
11	27	1	1	42	94	51	20	73	99	96	82
12	30	1	1	43	95	54	22	74	99	96	84
13	33	2	1	44	95	57	23	75	99	96	85
14	36	2	1	45	96	59	25	76	99	97	86
15	40	3	1	46	96	64	27	77	99	97	87
16	44	3	1	47	96	65	29	78	99	97	88
17	48	4	1	48	97	66	32	79	99	97	89
18	50	4	1	49	97	69	33	80-81	99	98	90
19	53	5	1	50	97	71	36	82	99	98	91
20	57	6	1	51	98	73	39	83-84	99	98	92
21	60	7	1	52	98	75	42	85	99	98	93
22	63	8	2	53	98	77	44	86	99	98	94
23	65	9	2	54	98	79	46	87-88	99	99	94
24	68	10	2	55	98	81	49	89-90	99	99	95
25	71	12	3	56	99	82	51	91-94	99	99	96
26	73	13	3	57	99	83	53	95-100	99	99	97
27	75	14	4	58	99	85	56	101-108	99	99	98
28	77	16	4	59	99	86	58	109+	99	99	99
29	79	18	5	60	99	87	60				
30	81	21	5	61	99	88	62				

National Percentile Ranks

Hearing and Recording Sounds in Words

Summary Statistics					
Period	N	Range	Median	Mean	SD
Fall	318,382	0–37	30	27.83	8.40
Mid-Year	298,692	0–37	36	34.64	3.71
Year-End	299,083	0–37	37	35.78	2.72

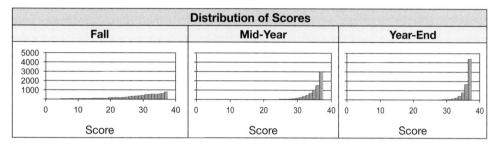

Distribution of Scores — Fall, Mid-Year, Year-End

Raw Score	National Percentile Rank			Raw Score	National Percentile Rank			Raw Score	National Percentile Rank		
	Fall	Mid-Year	Year-End		Fall	Mid-Year	Year-End		Fall	Mid-Year	Year-End
0-1	1	1	1	16	12	1	1	27	37	4	1
2-4	1	1	1	17	13	1	1	28	41	5	1
5-6	2	1	1	18	14	1	1	29	45	6	2
7-8	3	1	1	19	16	1	1	30	50	8	3
9	4	1	1	20	18	1	1	31	56	11	3
10	5	1	1	21	20	1	1	32	63	16	5
11	6	1	1	22	22	1	1	33	69	22	8
12	7	1	1	23	24	2	1	34	76	30	13
13	8	1	1	24	26	2	1	35	83	43	24
14	9	1	1	25	29	2	1	36	90	63	45
15	10	1	1	26	33	3	1	37	99	99	99

National Percentile Ranks

Text Reading Level

Summary Statistics

Period	N	Range	Median	Mean	SD
Fall	321,229	0–30	3	5.33	6.17
Mid-Year	301,502	0–30	12	13.6	7.65
Year-End	301,615	0–30	20	20.62	6.78

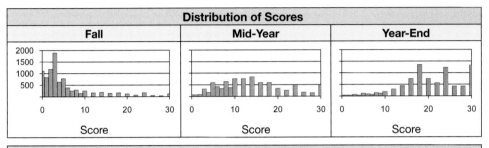

Distribution of Scores — Fall, Mid-Year, Year-End

National Percentile Ranks

Raw Score	National Percentile Rank			Raw Score	National Percentile Rank			Raw Score	National Percentile Rank		
	Fall	Mid-Year	Year-End		Fall	Mid-Year	Year-End		Fall	Mid-Year	Year-End
0	12	1	1	7	79	23	4	18	94	77	43
1	21	1	1	8	83	30	5	20	95	81	51
2	34	2	1	9	84	34	6	22	96	84	58
3	56	5	1	10	87	44	9	24	97	90	73
4	64	7	1	12	88	53	12	26	98	91	78
5	72	14	2	14	90	63	17	28	98	93	83
6	77	19	3	16	92	70	23	30	99	99	99

Appendix 7

OHIO WORD TEST — ADMINISTRATION SHEET

LIST A Practice Word can	LIST B Practice Word in	LIST C Practice Word see
and	ran	big
the	it	to
pretty	said	ride
has	her	him
down	find	for
where	we	you
after	they	this
let	live	may
here	away	in
am	are	at
there	no	with
over	put	some
little	look	make
did	do	eat
what	who	an
them	then	walk
one	play	red
like	again	now
could	give	from
yes	saw	have

OHIO WORD TEST SCORE SHEET

TEST SCORE: [ ] /20

STANINE GROUP: [ ]

Date: _____

Name: _____   School: _____

Recorder: _____   Classroom Teacher: _____

Record incorrect reponses.
Choose appropriate list of words.   ✔ (Check mark) Correct Response   • (Dot) No Response

LIST **A**	LIST **B**	LIST **C**
and	ran	big
the	it	to
pretty	said	ride
has	her	him
down	find	for
where	we	you
after	they	this
let	live	may
here	away	in
am	are	at
there	no	with
over	put	some
little	look	make
did	do	eat
what	who	an
them	then	walk
one	play	red
like	again	now
could	give	from
yes	saw	have

DUNCAN WORD TEST — ADMINISTRATION SHEET

LIST A Practice Word the	LIST B Practice Word a
and	to
my	I
it	is
up	you
Mum	for
in	went
on	are
Dad	he
go	no
me	can
we	was
big	said
of	come
going	see
she	but
little	here
have	got
out	not
down	am
they	some
what	that
there	with
came	all

DUNCAN WORD TEST SCORE SHEET
Use either list of words

Date: _____

Name: _____

Age: _____ Date of Birth: _____

TEST SCORE: | /23 |

Recorder: _____

STANINE GROUP:

Record incorrect responses beside word

LIST A	LIST B
and	to
my	I
it	is
up	you
Mum	for
in	went
on	are
Dad	he
go	no
me	can
we	was
big	said
of	come
going	see
she	but
little	here
have	got
out	not
down	am
they	some
what	that
there	with
came	all

References

Aman, M.G. and Singh, N.M. (1983). Specific reading disorders: Concepts of etiology reconsidered. In K.D. Gadow and I. Bader (Eds.) *Advances in Learning and Behavioural Disabilities*, Vol. 2: 1–47. Greenwich, CT: JAI Press.

Bissex, G. (1980). *GNYS AT WRK: A Child Learns To Write And Read*. Cambridge, MA: Harvard University Press.

Boocock, C. (1991). *Observing Children Write in the First Four Years of School*. Unpublished master's thesis, University of Auckland Library.

Boocock, C., McNaughton, S. and Parr, J.M. (1998). The early development of a self-extending system in writing. *Literacy Teaching and Learning, 3*(2): 41–59.

Brown, R.A. (1973). *First Language. The Early Stages*. Cambridge, MA: Harvard University Press.

Cazden, C.B. (2001). *Classroom Discourse: The Language of Teaching*. Portsmouth, NH: Heinemann Educational Books.

Chomsky, C. (1972). Stages in language development and reading exposure. *Harvard Educational Review, 22*: 1–33.

Clay, M.M. (1966). *Emergent Reading Behaviour*. Unpublished doctoral dissertation, University of Auckland Library.

——— (1967). The reading behaviour of five-year-old children: A research report. *New Zealand Journal of Educational Studies, 2*(1): 11–31.

——— (1968). A syntactic analysis of reading errors. *Journal of Verbal Learning and Verbal Behavior, 7*: 434–438.

——— (1969). Reading errors and self-correction behaviour. *British Journal of Educational Psychology, 39*: 47–56.

——— (1970a). Research on language and reading in Pakeha and Polynesian children. In D. K. Bracken and E. Malmquist (Eds.) *Improving Reading Ability Around The World*. Newark, DE: International Reading Association.

——— (1970b). Language skills: A comparison of Maori, Samoan and Pakeha children aged 5 to 7 years. *New Zealand Journal of Educational Studies*: 153–170.

——— (1971). Sentence Repetition: Elicited Imitation of a Controlled Set of Syntactic Structures by Four Language Groups. *Monograph of the Society for Research in Child Development, 36*, No. 143.

——— (1972a). *Reading: The Patterning of Complex Behaviour*. Auckland: Heinemann. (2nd ed. 1979).

——— (1972b). *The Early Detection of Reading Difficulties: A Diagnostic Survey*. Auckland: Heinemann. (2nd ed. 1979; 3rd ed. 1985).

——— (1972c). *Sand – the Concepts About Print Test*. Auckland: Heinemann.

——— (1974a). Orientation to the spatial characteristics of the open book. *Visible Language, 8*(3): 275–282.

——— (1974b). The development of morphological rules in children of differing language backgrounds. *New Zealand Journal of Educational Studies, 9*(2): 113–121.

——— (1975a). *What Did I Write?* Auckland: Heinemann.

——— (1975b). Learning to inflect English words. *Regional English Language Centre Journal, Singapore, 6*(1)1: 33–42.

——— (1976). Early childhood and cultural diversity. *The Reading Teacher* (January): 312–333.

——— (1979a). *The Early Detection of Reading Difficulties* (2nd ed.). Auckland: Heinemann.

——— (1979b). *Stones – the Concepts About Print Test*. Auckland: Heinemann.

——— (1979c). *Reading: The Patterning of Complex Behaviour*. Auckland: Heinemann.

——— (1982). *Observing Young Readers: Selected Papers*. Portsmouth, NH: Heinemann.

——— (1985). *The Early Detection of Reading Difficulties* (3rd ed.). Auckland: Heinemann.

——— (1987). *Writing Begins At Home*. Auckland: Heinemann.

——— (1989). Concepts about print: In English and other languages. *The Reading Teacher 42*(4): 268–277.

——— (1991). *Becoming Literate: The Construction of Inner Control.* Auckland: Heinemann.

——— (1993a). *Reading Recovery: A Guidebook for Teachers in Training.* Auckland: Heinemann.

——— (1993b). *An Observation Survey of Early Literacy Achievement.* Auckland: Heinemann.

——— (1998). *By Different Paths to Common Outcomes.* Auckland: Heinemann.

——— (2000a). *Running Records for Classroom Teachers.* Auckland: Heinemann.

——— (2000b). *Concepts About Print.* Auckland: Heinemann.

——— (2000c). *Follow Me, Moon – the Concepts About Print Test.* Auckland: Heinemann.

——— (2000d). *No Shoes – the Concepts About Print Test.* Auckland: Heinemann.

——— (2001). *Change Over Time in Children's Literacy Development.* Auckland: Heinemann.

——— (2002). *An Observation Survey of Early Literacy Achievement.* Second Edition. Auckland: Heinemann.

——— (2005a). *Literacy Lessons Designed for Individuals: Part One.* Auckland: Heinemann.

——— (2005b). *Literacy Lessons Designed for Individuals: Part Two.* Auckland: Heinemann.

——— (2010a). *How Very Young Children Explore Writing.* Auckland: Heinemann.

——— (2010b). *The Puzzling Code.* Auckland: Heinemann.

——— (2010c). *What Changes in Writing Can I See?* Auckland: Heinemann.

Clay, M.M., Gill, M., Glynn, T., McNaughton, T. and Salmon, K. (1983). *Record of Oral Language and Biks and Gutches.* Auckland: Heinemann.

Clay, M.M., Gill, M., Glynn, T., McNaughton, T. and Salmon, K. (2007). *Record of Oral Language.* Auckland: Heinemann.

Clay, M.M. and Imlach, R.H. (1971). Juncture, pitch and stress as reading behaviour variables. *Journal of Verbal Behaviour and Verbal Learning, 10*: 133–139.

Clay, M. M. (2003) *Le sondage d'observation en lecture-écriture.* Adaptation : Gisèle Bourque. Montréal: Chenelière Éducation.

Clay, M. and Nig Uidhir, G. (2006). *Áis mheasúnaithe sa luathlitearthacht: treoir ar mhúinteoirí,* Carroll Education Ltd.

Clough, M., McIntyre, J. and Cowey, W. (1990). *The Canberra Word Test.* University of Canberra, Australia: Schools and Community Centre.

Croft, A.C. and Mapa, L. (1998). *Spell-Write: An Aid to Writing and Spelling.* (Rev. ed.) Wellington: New Zealand Council for Educational Research.

D'Agostino, J.V. (2012). Technical review committee confirms highest NCRTI ratings for Observation Survey of Early Literacy Achievement. *Journal of Reading Recovery, 11*(2): 53–56.

D'Agostino, J.V. (2012). US norms for tasks of An Observation Survey of Early Literacy Achievement. Columbus, OH: The Ohio State University International Data Evaluation Center.

Day, H.D. and Day, K.C. (1980). The reliability and validity of the Concepts About Print and Record of Oral Language. Resources in Education, EP 179 932. Arlington, VA: ERIC Document Reproduction Service.

Denton, C. A., Ciancio, D. J. and Fletcher, J. M. (2006). Validity, reliability, and utility of the Observation Survey of Early Literacy Achievement. *Reading Research Quarterly, 41*(1): 8–34.

Department of Education (1985). *Reading in the Junior Classes.* Wellington: Learning Media.

Duncan, S. and McNaughton, S. (2001). Research Note: Updating the Clay Word Test. *New Zealand Journal of Educational Studies,* December, Vol. 2.

Dyson, A.H. (1997). *Writing Superheroes: Contemporary Childhood, Popular Culture and Classroom Literacy.* New York: Teachers College Press.

Elkonin, D.B. (1973). USSR. In J. Downing (Ed.) *Comparative Reading*: 551–580. New York: Macmillan.

Elley, W., Ferral, H. and Watson, V. (2011). *Star Reading Test 2nd Edition.* Wellington: New Zealand Council for Educational Research.

Escamilla, K. (1992). *Descubriendo la Lectura: An Application of Reading Recovery in Spanish*. Report for the Office of Educational Research and Improvement. Washington, DC.

Escamilla, K., Andrade, A.M., Basurto, A.G.M. and Ruiz, O. (1996). *Instrumento de Observacion de los Logros de la Lecto-Escritura Inicial (A Spanish Reconstruction of An Observation Survey: A Bilingual Text)*. Portsmouth, NH: Heinemann.

Fernald, Grace M. (1943). *Remedial Techniques in Basic School Subjects*. New York: McGraw-Hill.

Ferreiro, E. and Teberosky, A. (1982). *Literacy Before Schooling*. Portsmouth, NH: Heinemann.

Genishi, C. (1982). Observational research methods for early childhood education. In B. Spodek *Handbook of Research in Early Childhood Education*. New York: The Free Press.

Girling-Butcher, W., Phillips, G. and Clay, M.M. (1991). Fostering independent learning. *The Reading Teacher, 49*(9): 694–697.

Gómez-Bellengé, F.X., Rodgers, E., Schulz, M. and Wang, C. (2005). Examination of the validity of the Observation Survey with a comparison to the ITBS. Paper presented at the Annual Meeting of the American Educational Research Association, Montreal, Quebec, Canada.

Goodman, Y. (Ed.), (1990). *How Children Construct Literacy: Piagetian Perspectives*. Newark, DE: International Reading Association.

Goodman, Y.M. and Burke, C. (1972). *The Reading Miscue Inventory*. New York: Macmillan.

Hart, B. and Risley, T.R. (1999). *The Social World of Children Learning to Talk*. Baltimore, MD: Paul Brookes.

Huggins, I., Matczuk, A., Tolentino, J. and Kniskern, J. (2008). Developing Canadian Norms for An Observation Survey of Early Literacy Achievement.

Holliman, A. J., Hurry, J. and Douëtil, J. (2010). Standardisation of the Observation Survey in England and Wales, UK. University of London, London: Institute of Education.

Hurry, J. (1996). What is so special about Reading Recovery? *The Curriculum Journal, 7*(8): 93–108.

Johns, J. (1980). First Graders' Concepts About Print. *Reading Research Quarterly, 15*(4): 529–549.

Johnston, P.H. (1996). *Knowing Literacy: Constructive Literacy Assessment*. York, ME: Stenhouse.

——— (2000). *Running Records: A Self-tutoring Guide*. Portland, ME: Stenhouse.

Koefoed, B., Boocock, C. and Wood, J. (1999). *An Observation Survey, The Video: Guidenotes*. Auckland: Heinemann.

Koefoed, B. and Watson, B. (1999). *An Observation Survey, The Video*. Auckland: Heinemann.

Kress, G. (2000). *Early Spelling: Between Convention and Creativity*. London: Routledge.

Levy, P. and Goldstein, H. (1984). *Introduction to Tests in Education: A Book of Critical Reviews*. London: Academic Press.

Lyman, H.B. (1963). *Test Scores and What They Mean*. Englewood Cliffs, NJ: Prentice-Hall.

Mattingly, I.G. (1972). Reading, the linguistic process, and linguistic awareness. In J.F. Kavanagh and I.G. Mattingly (Eds.) *Language by Ear and Eye*. Cambridge, MA: MIT Press.

——— (1979). The psycholinguistic basis for linguistic awareness. In M.L. Kamil and A.J. Moe (Eds.) *Twenty-eighth Yearbook of the National Reading Conference*: 257–271.

McKenzie, M. (1989). *Journeys Into Literacy*. Huddersfield: Schofield and Sims.

Ministry of Education (1996). *The Learner as a Reader*. Wellington: Learning Media.

——— (1997). *School Entry Assessment: A Guide for Teachers*. Wellington: Learning Media.

——— (1998). *School Entry Assessment: The First National Picture*. Compiled by A. Gilmore. Wellington: Ministry of Education.

——— (2001). *School Entry Assessment June 1997– December 2000*. Wellington: Learning Media.

——— (2003). *Effective Literacy Practice in Years 1 to 4*. Wellington: Learning Media.

——— (2009). *Learning Through Talk: Oral Language in Years 1 to 3*. Wellington: Learning Media.

Morrow, L.M. (1989). *Literacy Development in the Early Years: Helping Children Read and Write*. Englewood Cliffs, NJ: Prentice-Hall.

National Center on Response to Intervention (2012). Screening Charts. Retrieved April 3, 2012, from http://www.rti4success.ort/screeningTools

Neale, M. (1958). *The Neale Analysis of Reading Ability*. London: Macmillan. Revised in 1988 by the Australian Council for Educational Research, Melbourne, Australia, and also in 1989 by the National Foundation for Educational Research-Nelson, Slough, England.

New Zealand Council for Educational Research (NZCER) (1981). *Burt Word Reading Test*. Wellington: New Zealand Council for Educational Research.

Paley, V. (1981). *Wally's Stories*. Cambridge, MA: Harvard University Press.

Perkins, K. C. (1978). Developmental observations of kindergarten children's understanding in regard to Concepts About Print, language development, and reading behavior. Denton, TX: College of Education, Texas Woman's University.

Peters, M.L. (1970). *Success in Spelling*. Cambridge: Cambridge Institute of Education.

Phillips, G. (2001). Personal communication with author.

Pinnell, G.S., Lyons, C.A., DeFord, D.E., Bryk, A.S. and Seltzer, M. (1994). Comparing instructional models for the literacy education of high-risk first graders. *Reading Research Quarterly, 29*(1): 8–39.

Pinnell, G.S., Lyons, C.A., Young, P. and DeFord, D.E. (1987). The Reading Recovery Program in Ohio, Volume VI (Technical Report). Columbus, OH: The Ohio State University.

Pinnell, G.S., McCarrier, A. and Button, K. (1990). Constructing literacy in urban kindergartens: Progress report on the kindergarten early literacy project. Report No. 10 (MacArthur Foundation). Columbus, OH: The Ohio State University.

Rau, C. (1998). *He Mātai Āta Titiro Ki Te Tūtukitanga Mātātupu Pānui, Tuhi*. The Maori reconstruction of *An Observation Survey of Early Literacy Achievement*. Ngaruawahia: Kia Ata Mai Educational Trust.

Read, C. (1975). *Children's Categorization of Speech Sounds in English*. Urbana, IL: National Council of Teachers of English.

Robinson, S.M. (1973). *Predicting Early Reading Progress*. Unpublished master's thesis, University of Auckland Library.

Rowe, K.J. (1997). Factors affecting students' progress in reading: Key findings from a longitudinal study. In S.L. Swartz and A.F. Klein (Eds.) *Research in Reading Recovery*. Portsmouth, NH: Heinemann.

Rowe, K.J. and Rowe, K.S. (1999). Investigating the relationship between students' *attentive-inattentive* behaviours in the classroom and their literacy progress. *International Journal of Educational Research, 31*(1–2): 1–38 (whole issue).

Smith, F. (1978). *Understanding Reading*. 2nd ed. New York: Holt Rinehart and Winston.

Stallman, A.C. and Pearson, P.D. (1990). Formal measures of early literacy. In L.M. Morrow and J.K. Smith (Eds) *Assessment for Instruction in Early Literacy*. Englewood Cliffs, NJ: Prentice-Hall.

Stuart, M. (1995). Prediction and qualitative assessment of five- and six-year-old children's reading: A longitudinal study. *British Journal of Educational Psychology, 65*: 287–296.

Sylva, K. and Hurry, J. (1995). The effectiveness of Reading Recovery and phonological training for children with reading problems. *Full Report prepared for the School Curriculum and Assessment Authority*. London: Thomas Coram Research Unit.

Vernon, S. and Ferreiro, E. (1999). Writing development: A neglected variable in the consideration of phonological awareness. *Harvard Educational Review, 69*(4): 395–415.

——— (2000). Writing and phonological awareness in Spanish-speaking kindergarteners. *Harvard Educational Research Newsletter*, February 1–2, Cambridge, MA.

Watson, S. and Clay, M.M. (1975). Oral reading strategies of third form students. *New Zealand Journal of Educational Studies, 10*(1): 43–50.

Wells, G. (1986). *The Meaning Makers: Children Learning Language and Using Language to Learn*. Portsmouth, NH: Heinemann Educational Books.

Index